SINGAPORE
PERSPECTIVES 2015
Choices

SINGAPORE PERSPECTIVES 2015
Choices

Edited by

Carol Soon
Hoe Su Fern

Institute of Policy Studies, Singapore

LKY Lee Kuan Yew
School of Public Policy
National University of Singapore

iPS Institute of
Policy Studies

World Scientific

Published by

World Scientific Publishing Co. Pte. Ltd.
5 Toh Tuck Link, Singapore 596224
USA office: 27 Warren Street, Suite 401-402, Hackensack, NJ 07601
UK office: 57 Shelton Street, Covent Garden, London WC2H 9HE

British Library Cataloguing-in-Publication Data
A catalogue record for this book is available from the British Library.

SINGAPORE PERSPECTIVES 2015
Choices

ISBN 978-981-4696-83-8 (pbk)

In-house Editor: Sandhya Venkatesh

Contents

Preface

JANADAS DEVAN

Fifty years ago today, our future was uncertain. We didn't know it then, but on January 26, 1965, the Singapore Cabinet debated a paper that Mr Lee Kuan Yew had written on possible constitutional rearrangements in Malaysia.

1964 had been tense: the People's Action Party (PAP) had decided to contest the Malaysian General Election in April 1964, but won only one seat among the nine it contested in Peninsula Malaysia. In July 1964, and again in September, Singapore exploded in race riots, with a total of 36 people killed and 560 injured. Singapore and Kuala Lumpur clashed repeatedly — in the Federal Parliament, in the media and on the ground. Singapore saw no economic advantage in merger — the reason why we joined Malaysia in the first place, believing a small island state could not survive without a hinterland. For example, the Economic Development Board had to seek permission from Kuala Lumpur to award pioneer certificates to prospective investors here, entitling them to tax-free status for five to 10 years. In the two years we were in Malaysia, only two out of 69 such applications were approved, and one came with so many restrictions it amounted to a rejection.

Dr Goh Keng Swee recounts in his oral history a conversation he had with a World Bank expert who was advising Kuala Lumpur and Singapore on the common market. "Suppose [the Malaysian Finance Minister Tan Siew Sin] does not play the game and the common market does not get off the ground — what happens?" Dr Goh recalls asking the World Bank expert.

The expert answered presciently thus: "In that event, Mr Minister, it's not the common market which should be in danger; the whole concept of Malaysia would be in danger."

By December 1964, the Malaysian Prime Minister Tunku Abdul Rahman was already sounding an ominous warning: "If the politicians of various colours and tinges and flashes in Singapore disagree with me, the only solution is a breakaway," he said in a speech to the Medical College in Singapore. Ten days later, on December 19, he spelt out to Mr Lee privately what he meant by "breakaway": Singapore was to be "in partnership, independent, but part of the peninsula". In other words, a confederation, not a federation.

The Singapore government was to possess all the powers it had in the years of self-government between 1959 and 1963 prior to joining Malaysia. Kuala Lumpur would be in charge of only defence and external relations, as the British had been, and both governments would share responsibility for security in an Internal Security Council. Singapore citizens would not participate in politics beyond the island and Malaysian citizens would withdraw from political activity on the island. This was the substance of the paper Mr Lee presented to his Cabinet on January 26, 50 years ago today. Mr S Rajaratnam and Dr Toh Chin Chye vehemently opposed the proposals but the majority of the Cabinet supported the idea, according to Mr Lee. They saw disengagement as a way to avoid bloodshed.

But the proposal floundered for a number of reasons:

One, it soon became obvious that the Tunku wanted Singapore out of the Malaysian Parliament altogether. But he wanted Singapore to contribute to the cost of Malaysian defence, with a portion of Singapore's tax revenue going to Kuala Lumpur. There could be no taxation without representation, Mr Lee told the Tunku. We cannot become a colony in Malaysia.

Two, Kuala Lumpur wanted Singapore out of Malaysian politics but it wasn't prepared for the *quid pro quo*: Malaysia out of Singapore politics. Their fundamental precondition, Mr Lee was to write in his memoirs decades later, "was that, not only in Malaysia but even in Singapore itself, the PAP should stay out of the Malay world and leave it entirely to UMNO to deal with the Malays... even in Singapore".

And finally, the British got wind of the talks and scuttled everything. They were defending Malaysia against Indonesia's "Confrontation" and they weren't prepared to see their rear disintegrate while they defended the frontier. Instead of a looser confederation, they wanted a national government, with PAP ministers in the federal cabinet.

But what would have happened if the British had not scuttled the confederation idea? There was a reasonable chance the two parties, Singapore and Kuala Lumpur, might have come to an agreement. We cannot say this with certainty 50 years later, but it is probably fortunate the confederation idea collapsed. It would have given us "one country, two systems" decades before Deng Xiaoping proposed it for Hong Kong. Only in this case, it would have been an arrangement between two peoples who had perhaps less in common than the Hongkongers have with the Chinese today — despite which, see what difficulty the Special Administrative Region has had.

In retrospect, it may seem obvious that with the confederation idea having collapsed by February 1965, separation six months later was inevitable. But there was nothing inevitable about any of it. As uncomfortable as the Malaysian leaders were with Singapore, there was always at the back of their minds a fear that a Singapore out of Malaysia was a worse possibility than a Singapore in Malaysia. Indeed, a few years after Separation, both the Tunku and Tun Abdul Razak were to express regret for having let Singapore go. And as glad as the entire Singaporean leadership — indeed almost all Singaporeans — were to become that Singapore had extricated itself from Malaysia, that wasn't the consensus view even within the PAP at that time. "Singapore shall forever be a sovereign democratic and independent nation," the Proclamation read on August 9, 1965. On August 8, there were many among the 10 who signed the Separation Agreement who doubted if Singapore should ever be an independent state, let alone be independent forever! The desire for independence came the day after, on August 10.

There were at least two views within the Singapore leadership then:

One, a group that felt that since the common market wasn't in the offing, merger was literally useless. Trying to make a political success of an arrangement that lacked an economic rationale was pointless. Dr Goh Keng Swee seems to have been the first Singaporean leader who arrived at this conclusion. He was instrumental in removing the albatross around our necks that Malaysia had become. Others who held this view included Mr E.W. Barker, who was to draft the Separation Agreement, and Mr Lim Kim San.

Two, a more pronounced political group that believed with every fibre of their being that Singapore was an inextricable part of Malaya, and they owed it to the millions they had mobilised in both East and West Malaysia to fight on, unbowed and dauntless, for a Malaysian Malaysia. Dr Toh and Mr

Rajaratnam, in particular, held this view, as did Mr Ong Pang Boon. They signed the Separation Agreement with a heavy heart, impelled more by loyalty to the movement and Mr Lee than conviction that Separation was the right course.

It is next to impossible for almost all of us here to understand the depth of these sentiments. "History with its flickering lamp stumbles along the trail of the past, trying to reconstruct its scenes, to revive its echoes, and kindle with pale gleams the passion of former days," Churchill once wrote.

Let me speak personally for a moment to try to revive some of these echoes. My father, Devan Nair, was the only PAP candidate to have won a seat in the 1964 Malaysian General Election. Therefore, when Separation came, he was the only Singaporean leader with a seat in the Malaysian Parliament by virtue of representing a constituency in the peninsula, not Singapore. Dr Goh had arranged with Tun Razak that no PAP Member of Parliament would be present in the Malaysian Parliament when it voted on the Separation Bill. Mr Devan Nair, however, attended and declared that Malaysia might have separated from Singapore but it had not separated from him. In a speech interrupted many times by the Government benchers, he spoke of "a wrench in the heart" and announced he would remain in Malaysia and continue fighting for a "Malaysian Malaysia".

Thus the PAP in Malaysia became the Democratic Action Party or DAP, now the largest opposition party in Malaysia. Contrary to rumours then (and now), this decision to remain behind in Malaysia was his and not that of the Singapore leadership. It took another two-and-a-half years for Mr Lee to persuade him to return to Singapore. Mr Devan Nair announced in May 1968 that he was resigning as DAP Secretary-General and would not re-contest his seat in the Malaysian Parliament in the next general election. He returned to Singapore and the NTUC in 1969. He was the last among Singapore's leadership of that time to accept that Separation was irreversible. He was 45 when he finally received his Singapore identity card. He had believed till then that he was Malayan.

So had all the founding leaders of Singapore, including Mr Lee. He had said on August 9, 1965, that he had fought for merger all his adult life and that he would always look back on that day as "a moment of anguish".

After the idea of a looser confederation had floundered in February 1965, Mr Lee had adopted a strategy fraught with enormous risk to himself and his colleagues, including the possibility he might have been bumped off, as then British Prime Minister Harold Wilson recognised. He decided to raise the stakes considerably: either the Malaysian leadership settled on our terms — a non-communal, multi-racial and multi-religious polity — or they had to let us "hive off", to use a phrase of the Tunku's. So Mr Lee backed the Malaysian Solidarity Convention that Dr Toh and Mr Rajaratnam had formed, linked up all the non-communal political parties in Malaysia and didn't let up on the campaign for a Malaysian Malaysia. If anyone tried to start another riot in Singapore, they would have to account for the possibility of riots spreading to all the urban centres in the peninsula.

In the meantime, Dr Goh, who had begun talks with Tun Razak on July 13 or thereabouts, told the Tunku's key lieutenants they should settle fast before Mr Lee became irretrievably committed to the Malaysian Solidarity Convention and won more support for the PAP, both at home and abroad in the Commonwealth. The Tunku himself had by then concluded that he wanted Singapore out of Malaysia and asked Tun Razak to pursue all options, including outright separation, with Dr Goh. Dr Goh, committed as he was by then to independence, took the bull by the horns, got a letter of authorisation from Mr Lee to pursue all options with the Malaysian leadership, ignored the idea of a looser confederation, plumped straight for Separation, suggested all the necessary constitutional instruments be put through the Malaysian Parliament on August 9 and insisted on absolute secrecy especially from the British. Within a little more than four weeks, a constitutional coup — or "negotiated separation" as the draughtsman of our independence, Mr Barker, put it in his oral history — was encompassed. I have said elsewhere that these months from January to August 1965 were the founding generation's finest hour — and I'm not referring only to the leaders of that time but also to the electorate that coalesced around them. For if Singaporeans had allowed themselves to be cowed, we might still have been offered "one country, two systems" as late as August 1965. Fortunately, our forefathers were a pride of lions led by lions.

Why do I recall this history? To remind ourselves that there was nothing inevitable about our founding. "What might have been and what has been point to one end, which is always present", the poet T.S. Eliot wrote. A people who forget their history will perish. I fear we might well become such a people. Raised in clover and accustomed to success, our elite especially have come to regard themselves as self-created, self-sustaining, self-perpetuating entities. What is, is; they have no antecedents; history is bunk. So they come to believe, for instance, that we were never vulnerable, that the vulnerabilities were myths, lies. Only a people who forget their history can delude themselves so.

What might have been and what has been point to one end, which is always present. Consider this: We came close to getting one country, two systems before we stumbled on Separation. All our founding leaders initially believed Singapore couldn't survive without a hinterland. They only abandoned the idea when it became obvious a common market with Malaysia wasn't on the cards. Even then, it hadn't occurred to them the world could be our hinterland; or if it had occurred to some of them, they didn't as yet know how to give effect to that vision. The notion of a "global city" was some years away; globalisation, decades. That we could be a hub in a variety of fields, that multi-national corporations could be our ticket, that we could be the centre of this, that or the other — none was obvious.

What might have been and what has been point to one end, which is always present. What might be that one end, which is always present? It means the paths not taken as well as the paths taken remain always possibilities — now. It means the risks avoided, the successes attained, the dangers circumvented, the achievements chanced upon — all are never ever wholly voided or erased. It means our history — for 50 years now a triumphant arc that bent always toward sunlit uplands and fresh pastures — our history can still turn tragic.

What might have been and what has been point to one end, which is always present. The one constant in our history has been our audacity. Pray that it may always remain so.

Acknowledgements

IPS is grateful to the following institutions for their support of Singapore Perspectives 2015 held on Monday, 26 January 2015.

Made possible by

Keppel Corporation

U Enterprise   **TEMASEK**

Supported by

BANYAN TREE

HOUSING &
DEVELOPMENT
BOARD

Institute of Technical Education

M P A
SINGAPORE

MCL Land

A Hongkong Land company

NYP NANYANG
THE INNOVATIVE POLYTECHNIC

NANYANG
TECHNOLOGICAL
UNIVERSITY

NUS
National University
of Singapore

NGEE ANN
P O L Y T E C H N I C

**REPUBLIC
POLYTECHNIC**

Supported by

Introduction

Looking Back to Look Forward

CAROL SOON AND HOE SU FERN

Singapore Perspectives 2015 took place during the year Singapore celebrates an important milestone in its national development after 50 years of independence. While Singapore has made widely lauded progress in political, economic and social advancement, she faces much uncertainty in the future due to changing demographics, geo-political developments and the emergence of regional competitors.

At this important milestone, it was apt that the conference turned to the past as a means to looking forward: What were the choices that our early leaders and pioneer generation had to make, in order to overcome the odds and obstacles as a newly independent nation state? What would the Singapore story be like if different choices were made and offbeat paths were taken? Are these decisions still viable and relevant choices for our continued survival in an increasingly complex and diverse world?

As Lee Kuan Yew once said, our survival is built on the will of our people to be a nation. It is our choice to come together as a tightly-knit community that has, and will enable us to do better than what we did before independence.

Hence, on 26 January 2015, more than 900 participants, including academics, researchers, policymakers, professionals from the private and non-profit sectors and tertiary students, came together at the Institute's flagship conference — befittingly titled "Choices" — and contemplated key choices made in society, economy and politics over the last 50 years to cultivate Singapore into a home that stirs pride and passion.

This book is the outcome of the presentations, debate and dialogue that took place at that coming-together. The presenters, all of whom are eminent thought leaders, went beyond reflecting on the critical decisions made in Singapore's past, to envision strategic paths that the nation should take in the future. The rich and varied discussions that ensued are a testament to Singapore's will to survive, and a glimpse into the shared hopes, aspirations and possibilities that will enable Singapore to progress and forge ahead together as a cohesive nation state in an increasingly uncertain world.

The first section of the book addresses the issue of sovereignty and it comprises contributions by Ambassador-at-Large and Policy Adviser of Ministry of Foreign Affairs Bilahari Kausikan and Shedden Professor of Strategic Policy Studies at the Australian National University Professor Evelyn Goh. In his chapter on sovereignty and survival, Mr Kausikan discussed the tenuity of sovereignty from the time of Singapore's merger and subsequent separation with Malaysia till now, and its implications for Singapore's survival as a small state. He proposed that although there is no one formula in staying relevant to the world, being extraordinary is an indispensable part of Singapore remaining as an enduring sovereign state in an unpredictable geo-political climate.

In her chapter, Professor Goh challenged conventional wisdom that sovereignty is static and a zero-sum game. Instead, she argued that territories and people all over the world are subject to multiple influences and systems of authority. She examined three possible future trajectories for Singapore: merger with neighbouring states or political entities; regional integration with ASEAN or East Asia; and hybrid sovereignty. She made the case for hybrid sovereignty as the most plausible option and discussed implications for policymakers.

Themed "Global City", the second section focuses on the Singapore economy, the model it adopted during the early years of independence and the model's sustainability in light of emerging regional players. In Chapter 3, Professor Tan Kong Yam of Nanyang Technological University presented key challenges to Singapore's economic future in light of the immense progress it has achieved till date based on the global-city model. He discussed how the survival of Singapore's economy hinges on her ability and nimbleness in managing discontents of her polity and risks. The two main strategic thrusts put forth in Professor Tan's chapter include providing targeted subsidies for the lowest 30% of the population and strengthening the mothership of Singapore. Similar to Professor Tan, Professor Linda Lim of the Stephen M. Ross School of Business at the University of Michigan adopted a long-term perspective in analysing imminent economic threats and opportunities faced by Singapore. She posited that rapidly changing global and national conditions (e.g., worldwide macroeconomic, technological, social and environmental changes) necessitate a strategy that is different from the global-city model, which has served Singapore well in the last 50 years. She put forth a compelling argument for a shift of focus to the region and social adjustments on the domestic front.

The proceedings for the paired debate on the motion "Should pragmatism be retained as Singapore's governing philosophy?" are presented in the third section of the book. The proposers for the motion were Professor Kishore Mahbubani, Dean of the Lee Kuan Yew School of Public Policy, and social entrepreneur Tong Yee, Director of The Thought Collective. *The Business Times*' Associate Editor Vikram Khanna and Associate Professor Eugene Tan of the Singapore Management University opposed the motion. The proposers and opposers argued the motion on philosophical, governance, economic and moral grounds.

The proposing team traced the history of pragmatism to societies and rulers developing pragmatism in their continual attempt to deliver a good life for their people, and made the point that the roots of pragmatism exist in Western, Indian and Chinese philosophies. Pointing to geopolitical, economic and social challenges, the proposing team warned that small states that stopped being pragmatic would have to cope with disastrous consequences. While recognising that pragmatism has been critical to the Singapore success story and should remain, the opposing team argued that it should not be the nation-state's governing philosophy. Although pragmatism is important, Vikram Khanna and Associate Professor Tan contended that it must be accompanied by idealism, inspiration, principle, conviction, and a moral compass. They bolstered their case by highlighting the ills of pragmatism — how it curtails discussion and innovation, discourages innovation due to fears of failure and encourages people to opt for expedient, tried and tested paths.

Chapter 6 details the proceedings for the ministerial dialogue featuring two ministers who entered politics almost two decades apart: Deputy Prime Minister (DPM) Teo Chee Hean and Chan Chun Sing, then Minister for Social and Family Development and Second Minister for Defence. Wide-ranging issues, including those on national identity, welfare policies, immigration, ageing population and increasing political diversity in society, were discussed during the session. From the role of history in the formation of Singapore's identity, the difficult choices made by the government pertaining to foreign workers and productivity to people's anxieties over changing societal values, the dialogue session provided intimate and candid insights into policymakers' concerns, aspirations and optimism for Singapore as it embarks on its next lap.

The final section in this book presents IPS' study on perceptions of Singapore's history, of which key findings were showcased in a two-part video presented at the conference.[1] Fifty local events — from the founding of modern Singapore to the general election in 2011 — were included in the study. Involving more than 1,500 Singaporeans, the study explored questions such as which Singapore stories were influential to them and why, with whom those stories resonated and, looking ahead, which types of narratives would inspire the current and future generations. In addition to the survey, focus group discussions were conducted with diverse groups of Singaporeans to gain deeper insights into which historical narratives had the strongest resonance and why.

The study offers a glimpse into the collective memory of Singaporeans. More importantly, the findings provide astute insights into the different strands of historical narratives entrenched in the Singaporean identity, and chronicle the Singapore journey over the past 50 years. The findings also give an idea of what could resonate as historical narratives for future generations of Singaporeans.

Ultimately, Singapore Perspectives 2015 highlights how, being Singaporean is a matter of choice; it is about "becoming" as much as it is of "being". It is not something that transcends time, history, place and culture. Rather, being

---

[1] The videos are archived at the Institute's YouTube channel and can be found at these links: https://www.youtube.com/watch?v=BxHAFMBzaFc and https://www.youtube.com/watch?v=IxYUDaViYN0

Singaporean is a complex and unstable production, never complete and always subject to the continuous play of choices. As S Rajaratnam famously put it, "being a Singaporean is not a matter of ancestry. It is [a matter of] conviction and choice".

Like the development of Singapore, Singapore Perspectives 2015 would not have been possible without the contribution of many people and parties. We are especially grateful to the IPS research assistants — Chang Zhi Yang, Mohammad Khamsya bin Khidzer, Tan Min Wei, Tay Ek Kiat — who helped conceptualised and finessed the theme. Our gratitude also goes to the speakers who gave unstintingly of their expertise and time. We would also like to thank the participants at the Singapore Perspectives conference for their incisive questions and comments. Their questions and comments served as important input for the speakers who expanded their presentations for publication in this book, for which we are thankful.

The smooth running of the conference would not have been possible without the IPS administration team. We extend our deepest appreciation to the students from the School of Interactive and Digital Media in Nanyang Polytechnic and their instructors for putting together two videos that showcased the findings of the study. Special thanks are also extended to Christopher Gee, Rachel Hoa, Chan Yi Ying and Dr Gillian Koh for coordinating the publication of this book, and to Leong Wenshan for copy-editing this volume.

1

Sovereignty

1

Sovereignty for Small States

BILAHARI KAUSIKAN

What does "sovereignty" mean to a small country such as Singapore? We did not seek independence but had independence thrust upon us. I have been told that Mr Lee Kuan Yew once said, "Small island states are a political joke." That quote implies a concept of sovereignty based on which our founding fathers sought independence within Malaysia rather than alone.

I suspect it was difficult for that generation to even conceive of Singapore as anything but a part of what was then called Malaya. Obviously, and thankfully, that concept of sovereignty was proved mistaken or was rendered mistaken by the Herculean efforts of our pioneer generation. And by that, I do not mean just our leaders, but our entire people.

The concept of sovereignty is constantly evolving. Rather than try to define the elephant, I propose to take its existence for granted and instead consider what sovereignty means to Singapore by analysing a single sentence, and that sentence is this: "Singapore is a small state located in South-east Asia."

This seems straightforward, but is it really? What do we mean by "small"? We are, of course, a physically small country and a moderately athletic person could walk across it in a day without too much difficulty. But as a trading centre, as a logistics hub, as a port and airport and as a financial centre, among other things, we are far from "small". In trade, connectivity and finance, among others, we loom quite large internationally, far larger than our physical size may lead one to expect.

Sir Stamford Raffles established modern Singapore as a trading centre in 1819. And I read somewhere that by 1898, or thereabouts, our trade was larger than that of Japan, larger than that of what was then called the Dutch East Indies, and was exceeded only by China. Some recent archaeological studies suggest that we may have been a significant trading centre since the 14th century, even before the concept of sovereignty in its current form existed.

Trade requires connectivity; it requires logistics and finance. Of course, today, we perform these functions at a far higher level of sophistication and complexity than in the past. But the point is that they are essentially similar functions and we have performed them as a British colony, as part of Malaysia and only in the past 50 years — which is but the blink of an eyelid in the sweep of history — as a sovereign and independent country.

There is, therefore, no reason to assume that sovereignty and independence are necessary conditions to enable us to perform such functions. We could conceivably do so even if our independence and sovereignty were, by some blunder of policy, accident of politics or malicious whim of the gods, severely compromised.

Size — physical size — does matter. And small states are intrinsically irrelevant to the workings of the international system. It is impossible to imagine a world without large countries such as the United States, China, India, Indonesia, Brazil or Russia, or even without medium-sized states such as Australia, Japan, France or Germany. But the world would probably get along fine without Singapore as a sovereign and independent country. After all, it has only had to put up with us for 50 years. For small states, relevance is not something that can be taken for granted, but rather an artefact — created by human endeavour, and once created, preserved by human endeavour. The creation and maintenance of relevance must be the overarching strategic objective of small states.

The majority of states are small. Slightly more than two decades ago, Singapore established the Forum of Small States (FOSS) at the United Nations; "small" being somewhat arbitrarily defined as having a population of 10 million or less. It now has 105 members out of a total UN membership of 193 states. The international relevance of many FOSS members is defined primarily by their vote within the UN. A vote in the UN is only that. It is not to be sneezed at but it is still only one vote. Singapore is exceptional as a small country in that our international identity and relevance is something more than just our UN vote. We have options beyond our single UN vote, and that is why we were able to establish FOSS in the first place.

How do we create relevance? There is no magic formula. What makes us relevant vis-à-vis country A may be irrelevant vis-à-vis country B and may become irrelevant to both A and B as well as C in a week or a month or a year or a decade. What is relevant will eventually become irrelevant and must therefore be continually refreshed.

The world is constantly changing and since the world will not change to suit our conveniences, we will have to constantly adapt to it. Since the future is unknowable, adaptation requires nimbleness of thought and action. Such thought and action need to be based on a clinical — some say cold-blooded — understanding of the world as it is and not as we think it ought to be. Even if we hope to change the world, we must first understand it without illusions because hope, however fervent, is never enough.

The bedrock of relevance is success. I have always told our Foreign Service Officers (FSOs) that if Singapore's foreign policy has been successful to some degree, it is not because of their good looks, it is not due to their natural charm, it is not due to the genius of their intellect. The most brilliant idea of a small country can be safely disregarded, if inconvenient, whereas the stupidest idea of a large country must be taken seriously. In fact, the stupider the idea the more seriously it must be taken because of the harm a large country can do. So if our FSOs succeed, it is only because Singapore as a country is successful. Singapore's success invests our ideas and actions with credibility.

Success must be defined, first of all, in economic terms. Will a barren rock ever be taken seriously? I know that it has become fashionable in certain circles to claim that economic success is not everything and that there are other worthy goals in life. I do not disagree as far as individuals are concerned. If any of our compatriots chooses to drop out of the rat race and devote his or her life to art or music or religion or even just to *lepak*, or relax, in one corner, I respect their choice and wish them well.

However, the country as a whole does not have this luxury. A world of sovereign states is, in fact, a rat race, and often a vicious one, in which the weak go to the wall. There can be no opting out for a sovereign state. To be crass, small countries will always have fewer options than large countries but rich small countries have more options than poor small countries and that tilts the scales in our favour. This is crucial because a small country cannot be only ordinarily successful. If we were no different from our neighbourhood, why should anyone want to deal with us rather than our larger neighbours who, moreover, are well endowed with natural resources? To be relevant, we have to be extraordinary. Being extraordinary is a strategic imperative.

And that brings me to the second part of the sentence with which I began. Singapore is not just a small country, but a small country in South-east Asia — not the South Pacific or South America or Europe or, thankfully, the Middle East. This seems obvious but I think this fact is nevertheless insufficiently appreciated, even by those who ought to know better.

A year or so ago, I was flabbergasted and disturbed when asked — asked in all seriousness and not just to take the mickey out of me (if it had been just to take the mickey out of me, it would have been acceptable) — by a Singaporean PhD candidate in political science why Singapore could not pursue a foreign policy akin to that of Denmark or Switzerland. The question aroused all my prejudices about the academic study of international relations. It makes a vast, and I thought glaringly obvious difference where a country is located. That a Singaporean PhD candidate, who presumably knew something about her own country as well as the subject she was studying, could ask such a question made me worry about the future of our country.

South-east Asia is not a natural region, by which I mean a region that can be defined by something intrinsic to itself. For example, Europe can be defined as heir to Christendom and the Roman Empire. The main characteristic of South-east Asia is diversity, which is another way of saying that there is nothing intrinsic to itself.

There are obvious differences of political form and levels of economic development. However, the most important diversities of South-east Asia are visceral: they are diversities of race, language and religion. These are the roots of political tension within and between the countries of South-east Asia. The Association of South-east Asian Nations (ASEAN) was set up with the intention, among other things, to mitigate these diversities to ensure a modicum of order and civility in interstate relationships in a region where this was not to be taken for granted. ASEAN has been reasonably successful. However, ASEAN can never entirely erase these primordial diversities because race, language and religion are the essence of core identities.

Singapore defines itself as a multiracial meritocracy and we organise ourselves on the basis of these principles. We are not perfect — there is no perfection to be found this side of heaven — but we take these principles seriously. They are what make Singapore, Singapore. They also make us extraordinary because our neighbours organise themselves on the basis of very different principles.

This is most obvious in the case of Malaysia. It was the irreconcilable contradiction between fundamentally different political philosophies — multiracial meritocracy in our case and Malay dominance politely enshrined in Article 153 of the Malaysian Constitution as "the special position of the Malays" — that made it impossible for us to remain in Malaysia. No matter how closely we cooperate — and despite occasional spats, we do cooperate very closely in many areas — it would be impossible for us to be part of Malaysia ever again unless Malaysia were to abandon its basic organising principle. And if you believe that will happen, there is a bridge I can let you have really cheap.

The essential issue is existential; not what we do, but what we are — a Chinese-majority country with neighbours whose own Chinese populations are typically less than fully welcome minorities and whose attitudes towards their own Chinese populations are too often projected upon us. The very existence of a Chinese-majority multiracial meritocracy that has been extraordinarily successful compared with its neighbours is often taken as an implicit criticism of differently-organised systems. That we are a tiny speck on the map and have hardly any history to speak of is an additional affront.

The intensity of such attitudes waxes and wanes; it manifests itself in different ways, at different times. But it never disappears because it is the structural consequence of the dynamic between different types of systems. Being extraordinary does not make us loved, but it is the price we must pay for survival and autonomy.

In different forms and various degrees, such attitudes exist throughout South-east Asia and in China, Japan and even Western countries such as Australia and the US. Examples spring to mind all too readily but diplomatic prudence does not permit me to elaborate, at least not too much.

Of course, none of this is intended to imply that we cannot work with our neighbours or any other country. Obviously we must, obviously we can and obviously we do and indeed, I dare say, we do so quite well. But these complexities are never going to go away and we ignore or deny them only at the peril of compromising our autonomy, that is to say, our sovereignty.

I believe that matters are going to get even more complicated because the external environment and our domestic environment are both changing and external and internal complexities will act and react with each other in ways that cannot be predicted.

There are already signs of foreign policy being used for partisan political purposes. This is probably inevitable. Domestic debates over foreign policy are not necessarily a bad thing provided that they take place within parameters defined by shared assumptions. Otherwise, it is playing with fire. At the very least, it degrades the nimbleness of our responses if we have to argue everything out anew from first principles.

Shared assumptions come naturally, almost unconsciously, to countries with long histories. But with only 50 years of shared history, I am not entirely confident that this is the case in Singapore. There is something of an intellectual vacuum that is being largely filled by nonsense.

We need to be better at educating ourselves about our own history. In my opinion, we are not doing a good enough job and the recent debates about our own political history are, unfortunately, notable only for their utter vacuity. What passes for critical thinking about our history is too often simply crying white if the establishment says black. Furthermore, social media exacerbates the situation by conflating information with opinion and treating both as entertainment.

As our domestic political environment becomes more complex with not only traditional political parties but also civil society organisations and advocacy groups espousing various causes contending in the policy space, opportunities for external influence will multiply.

Since the beginning of recorded history, states have always tried to influence each other, legitimately and openly through diplomacy but also oftentimes by covert means. The lines are not always clear and are likely to become even more blurred. The enthusiasm of some, mainly Western, diplomats to whip the heathen — that's us by the way — along the path of righteousness have already occasionally led them to cross the boundaries of legitimate diplomatic activity.

More fundamentally, market forces are creating economic spaces that transcend national boundaries, most notably between China and South-east Asia. This is to be welcomed on economic grounds but will have political and strategic consequences. It is redefining Westphalian notions of "state" and interstate relations and is putting stress on ASEAN as powerful centrifugal forces pull members in different directions.

As the only Chinese-majority country in South-east Asia, it could pose special challenges for Singapore. Already, Chinese diplomats and officials too often refer to Singapore as a "Chinese country". We politely, but firmly, tell them that they are mistaken. And we will continue to do so. But the implications are worth pondering.

CHAPTER 2

Singapore's Future in a World of Hybrid Sovereignty

EVELYN GOH

INTRODUCTION

This chapter examines Singapore's future as a sovereign state, especially against the background of challenges posed by globalisation. It is common to think about sovereignty in a relatively static and zero-sum way, as nation states enjoying monopoly control over their domestic affairs. However, the modes and practices of sovereignty have never been clear-cut throughout history. Singapore has experienced a relatively short encounter with the institution of sovereignty, which has been (a) traumatic because of its initial rapid succession from decolonisation to merger to fully fledged independence, and (b) intense because Singapore orchestrated its independent socio-economic development in a period when the forces of globalisation posed the most rapid, deep-set and wide-ranging challenges to conventional understandings of sovereignty. The chapter discusses three possible future trajectories for Singapore, all of which will have different implications for its sovereignty: (1) merger with neighbouring states or political entities, (2) regional integration with ASEAN or East Asia and (3) hybrid sovereignty. It argues that the third possibility is the most likely as it represents intensifying trends of sovereign practice over the last five decades of globalisation.

In 1965, thwarted in their preference for merger with the Malayan Federation, Singapore's founding leaders reluctantly chose sovereignty for the island state instead as the means by which to pursue their hard-won post-colonial independence. Fifty years of successful nation-building followed, but during this period, the world also changed rapidly and significantly. Most notably, technological advances have shrunk both time and distance, enabling far greater interaction, connectivity and interdependence among states, businesses and people around a globalising world. The twin consequences are that even as political and economic competition has intensified for states and corporations operating beyond national borders, the need for cooperation has also grown in the face of transboundary threats such as pollution, pandemics and terrorism. This chapter considers Singapore's future as a sovereign state in light of the myriad challenges posed by globalisation. It asks whether Singapore would need to consider again becoming part of a larger entity in order to ride future waves of change, what entity this might be and with what implications for Singapore's sovereignty.

To answer these questions, we first need to consider what sovereignty means. The basic concept of sovereignty is of nation states enjoying monopoly control over their domestic affairs. Scholars trace the modern system of sovereign states to the 1648 Peace of Westphalia, which ended the Thirty Years' War in Europe by trying to replace mixed feudal and religion-based polities with states that operated on the agreed principle of political self-determination, legal equality and non-intervention in internal affairs.[1] Subsequently adopted by post-colonial states and the United Nations in the 20th century, this "Westphalian" model of sovereignty is thus grounded in the understanding that "states exist in specific territories, within which domestic political authorities are the sole arbiters of legitimate behaviour" (Krasner, 1999, p. 20).[2] Sovereign states enjoy the twin rights to be free from external interference and to be recognised as autonomous agents in the international system that can interact with and enter into legal agreements with each other.

It is common to think about sovereignty in a zero-sum way; a political entity either has it, or it does not. For instance, in July 1971, the Republic of China, or Taiwan, lost its status as a sovereign state when a majority of

---

[1] For an overview of the evolution of European state systems from the ancient Greek city-states to 1945, see Reus-Smit, C. (1999), *The Moral Purpose of the State: Culture, Social Identity, and Institutional Rationality in International Relations*, Princeton, NJ: Princeton University Press.

[2] Krasner, S. D. (1999). *Sovereignty: Organized Hypocrisy*. Princeton, NJ: Princeton University Press.

member states in the United Nations General Assembly voted in favour of recognising the People's Republic of China on the mainland as the sovereign authority over China. The violation of sovereign independence is also regarded in international law as the key just cause for waging wars. Hence, for example, the only two notable international coalitions that were marshalled for collective defence since 1945 were the UN-sanctioned coalitions that intervened after North Korea invaded South Korea in 1950 and after Iraq invaded Kuwait in 1991. And yet, the modes and practices of sovereignty have never been clear-cut throughout history. In practice, sovereignty has not been a zero-sum condition. Indeed, many forms of external intervention into states' internal affairs — not just through war, but also through political dependence and the influence of multinational corporations and international organisations for example — are becoming increasingly common. As a result, one scholar has characterised sovereignty as a form of "organised hypocrisy" because the modern nation-state system appears to be based on an informal acceptance of the contradiction between ideal and practice (Krasner, 1999, p. 20).[3]

Furthermore, sovereignty has neither been understood nor practised in a static sense. The criteria for sovereignty have evolved. Initially, sovereign status was tied primarily to territorial control. For instance, the government of the United States under Thomas Jefferson acknowledged the French Revolutionary authorities in 1792 regardless of its radical character on the basis that the state continued to maintain effective control of France. But from the 20th century onwards, greater emphasis was given to a state's capacity to fulfil international commitments, especially regarding property rights. In the 1920s, many major states refused to recognise the Soviet regime that came to power following the Russian Revolution because the latter refused to fulfil the international legal duty of a sovereign state in compensating for foreign property that it had seized during the revolution. More recently, after the Cold War, the demand that some states must desist from suppressing their peoples has rendered sovereignty even more "conditional", as evidenced by the NATO-led intervention in Kosovo to protect civilians in 1999 and various UN-authorised operations to supply humanitarian aid and/or effect regime change in Somalia (1992), Haiti (1994) and Rwanda (1993–96). In the 2000s, the Responsibility to Protect doctrine mooted at the UN explicitly

---

[3] Ibid.

proposed that if a state failed to protect its population from genocide, war crimes, crimes against humanity and ethnic cleansing, it would forfeit aspects of its sovereignty, and the international community might be obliged to intervene, as subsequently happened in Kenya (2007–08), Côte d'Ivoire (2011), Libya (2011) and the Central African Republic (2013).

Significantly too, trends in sovereign practice have not developed in a linear fashion. Territories and peoples have been constantly subject to or chosen multiple systems of authority. The key example is Europe which, after 350 years of negotiating and fighting viciously over the contours of sovereignty since the treaties of Westphalia in 1648, opted to pool their hard-won individual autonomy in economic, military and political matters in the wake of two hot world wars and one Cold War. Sub-state entities (Scotland, Catalonia) seek independence even today, and it remains possible that the Union may disintegrate in the face of systemic financial crises.

SINGAPORE'S EXPERIENCE

Singapore has had a relatively short encounter with the institution of sovereignty. On the one hand, this encounter has been traumatic. Reflecting the ontological as well as political challenges facing new states emerging out of European colonialism, Singapore's journey to sovereign statehood involved a rapid succession from decolonisation to merger to fully-fledged independence. As this volume suggests, being Singaporean is a matter of choice. However, in 1965, this was largely viewed as a second, inadvertent choice. In the run-up to 1963, the choice of Singapore's pioneer leaders had been to become Malaysian — to have independence as a federal state in Malaysia. The failure of this experience forced Singapore's leaders and people to construct an alternative "imagined community" as Singaporeans, within an autonomous sovereign state based on racial equality.[4]

On the other hand, Singapore's experience has also been remarkably intense because Singapore orchestrated its independent socio-economic development

---

[4] The term coined by sociologist Benedict Anderson (2006) for the deliberate processes by which nationalism is created and sustained by populist movements, imperialist powers as well as post-colonial nation states.
Anderson, B. (2006). *Imagined Communities: Reflections on the Origins and Spread of Nationalism* (rev. ed.). London: Verso.

during a period when the forces of globalisation posed the most rapid, deep-set and wide-ranging challenges to conventional understandings of sovereignty. From the 1950s to 1970s, many newly independent states faced interference in their domestic affairs because of the ideological conflicts of the Cold War between capitalist and communist powers and parties. Within the capitalist world economy, the rise of multinational corporations (MNCs) operating across state boundaries (such as ExxonMobil, Unilever, General Motors, Shell, IBM), many with annual revenues bigger than the gross domestic products of large developing countries, seemed to fatally undermine state autonomy.[5]

Increasing economic interdependence also rendered national industrialising economies like Singapore vulnerable to external shocks over which they had no sovereign control. For example, the 1971 "Nixon shock" when President Richard Nixon ended the US dollar's convertibility with the international gold standard of international currency exchange and forced world currencies into an initially turbulent "floating system", the 1973–74 "oil crisis" when the Arab members of the Organisation of Petroleum Exporting Countries (OPEC) declared an embargo and drove oil prices up 400 per cent, and the 2008–09 global financial crisis triggered by the sub-prime mortgage crisis in the United States. The last 50 years have also seen the proliferation of layers of international and global governance with which sovereign states have had to engage and cede some autonomy, among others, the UN and its multiple legal and political bodies, institutions and regulatory regimes in trade (the General Agreement on Tariffs and Trade, the World Trade Organisation (WTO) and regional free trade agreements); finance (the International Monetary Fund or IMF); the World Bank; the Group of 8 (G8); the Group of 20 (G20); regional development banks; environment (the UN Conference on Environment and Development, the Framework Convention on Climate Change); and international law (various international tribunals for war crimes, the European Court of Justice, the International Criminal Court). Over this time, nation states have also faced the rise of security threats that genuinely span the globe — the prospect of nuclear annihilation, the long-drawn effects of uncontrolled climate change, financial as well as pathological contagions and the spectre of networks of terrorists and other violent extremists.

---

[5] See examples in Anderson, S., & Cavanagh, J. (2000). *Top 200: The Rise of Corporate Global Power*. Washington, DC: Institute for Policy Studies.

In spite of the trauma and the speed and intensity of globalisation pressures, Singapore has been agile in responding to the complexities and changes in practices of sovereignty over the last 50 years. And for a number of reasons outlined below, I would argue that Singapore's future experience of sovereignty could be exciting and promising.

SOVEREIGNTY TRENDS

To consider how Singapore might best leverage and practise its sovereignty in the future, it is useful first to understand how globalisation has already impacted upon sovereignty over the past 50 years. As observed above, stark autonomy (in the sense of being left alone by other states and international actors) has never been achievable in its ideal state. However, what globalisation has done is to undermine significantly the coincidence of authority and territory assumed within the Westphalian notion of sovereignty. States in the contemporary international system face two simultaneous pressures to:

a) return to a prior order within which a territory is subject to multiple systems of rule; but also to

b) leapfrog into a new order that transcends territorial and national boundaries all together.

The trends of sovereign practice over the last five decades have been shaped by globalisation in three key ways. First, globalisation has greatly intensified interdependence between states, in addition to the requirements for collective action among them. While it is a truism that international interdependence obliges individual states to work together to achieve their objectives, the technology and connectivity at the heart of globalisation have reduced temporal frames and de-spatialised international interactions to an unprecedented degree. As a result, governments are unable to govern effectively without collective action with other states and international actors, and this requirement may encroach upon autonomous national authority. For Singapore over the past 20 years, globalisation has exacerbated direct threats to the social well-being of Singaporeans, particularly in the form of severe transboundary pollution and pandemics like SARS and avian influenza. The key challenges posed in these experiences have been in the realm of how to achieve effective cooperation with other states to manage the problems. Such effective cooperation often entails some interference in the domestic affairs of other states (such as Indonesia's political-economic arrangements and policies affecting the use of commercial agricultural land in the management of forest fires that cause haze).

The imperative for collective action, while not entirely new, is exacerbated by the growing range and intensity of transnational threats, which may arise from state-sponsored or non-state actors in multiple world locations and working from diverse motives. For example, the September 2001 terrorist attacks in the United States highlighted how radical Islamic terrorist networks have been created out of disparate groups of local insurgents, globetrotting ideologues, mercenaries and foreign freedom fighters, sometimes — as in the case of the Afghan mujahideen — ironically funded by the American Central Intelligence Agency during the Cold War. To tackle the spread of such networks, or other insidious and amorphous threats such as cyber attacks on key state agencies, different states must give up some degree of autonomy to share intelligence resources, coordinate military action or policing policies, and cooperate to develop international rules to monitor, deter and punish offenders. Similarly, threats to economic prosperity (most evident in financial crises and contagions) cannot be tackled at the level of individual state policy alone: during the 1997 Asian financial crisis, for example, regional countries sought help from the IMF, which entailed severe conditionalities that impacted on their sovereignty over fiscal and monetary policies. But many Asian countries also reached out to bilateral lenders like the United States, and ASEAN also cooperated with China, Japan and South Korea to begin to develop an East Asian system of emergency currency swap arrangements (i.e., the Chiang Mai Initiative).

Second, globalisation has facilitated the diffusion of international authority away from the state. Nearly two decades ago, the international political economist Susan Strange warned that the state was losing the tug of war with the market — globalisation meant that state authority was undermined by the "accelerated integration of national economies into one single global market" (Strange, 1996, pp. 13–14)[6] and by the rise of non-state actors such as international corporations and organised criminal networks. As observed above, the rise of MNCs and recurring systemic shocks within the global

---

[6] Strange, S. (1996). *The Retreat of the State: The Diffusion of Power in the World Economy*. Cambridge: Cambridge University Press.

economy have exposed the limits of individual state authority. To meet the needs of regulation and governance associated with markets and other collective action problems, state authority has disaggregated "upwards" towards supranational bodies like WTO, IMF and G20. For effective implementation and because of more plural political orders, state authority has also diffused "downwards" towards sub-national groupings like local governments, non-governmental organisations (NGOs) and key individuals.

Finally, globalisation has also created unprecedented opportunities for subcontracting traditional functions of the sovereign state. The key functions and services of the state are increasingly tradable. For instance, mercenaries are an old phenomenon most recently revamped in the form of private military companies like Blackwater and DynCorp. Small states sell their country-code top-level domain names (such as .tv) for profit. Government-to-government service subcontracting is common. For example, Britain's Privy Council remains the highest court of appeal for many Commonwealth countries, including Singapore, while the Solomon Islands asked for direct law enforcement intervention from the Australian-led Regional Assistance Mission to Solomon Islands (RAMSI) in 2003. Foreign government-owned corporations are also building industrial and technology cities in China and providing social and legal services, and China recently contracted the US Federal Aviation Administration to train pilots and write the rules for China's national aviation.

Together, these trends have rendered state authority more "hybrid". In the face of globalisation, contemporary states enjoy, at best, hybrid sovereignty in the sense that the state's autonomy and authority now vary depending on the issue area and are not fixed over time. In many issue areas, sovereignty claims are resolutely not absolute any more (if they ever have been). As discussed above, part of the rationale lies in required collective action for securing public goods or establishing agreed governance frameworks. Such positive motivations often result in states voluntarily ceding some degree of autonomy in exchange for the stable expectations and common interests that cooperation brings. Yet there are other arenas in which states find their sovereignty subordinated by the intervention of more powerful states or international regimes, institutions or organisations. This may either be involuntary or a necessary compromise in order to participate in global political-economic exchange. For example, in many financial sub-sectors including currency valuation, insurance and banking, countries like Singapore that are active trading nations and global financial hubs must ascribe to multiple layers of international regulations, take into account the vagaries of domestic politics in major economies and be ready to submit to legal investigation and arbitration in international courts.

In sum, hybrid sovereignty is marked by variegation, cooperation and some subordination. Within the variegated landscape of hybrid sovereignty, state actors interested in maintaining sovereign control over vital issues must focus on three skill sets. First, they need to pay more attention now to control over networks — of finance, information, raw material flows, cyberspace — rather than control over physical territory per se. Transactions still take place in physical space of course, but the precise locations are now more ambiguous and dispersed depending on purposes. Similarly, understanding flows — of money, goods, information, even of people — across physical and political borders is more salient than being able to police political boundaries themselves.

Second, states also have to grapple with multiple opposing forces arising from globalisation. Globalisation's threats to sovereignty do not meet linear responses. For instance, transboundary threats from non-state actors, rather than generating transnational collective action in response, may often reify the individual state's authority. A good example here is how the George W. Bush administration used the September 11 terrorist attacks to bolster US laws against terrorism at home and abroad, and to launch traditional state-led military campaigns against other states harbouring terrorists and weapons of mass destruction. Another example is how the increasing denationalisation of the national economy and the easing of borders for labour flows can lead to the renationalisation of immigration and citizenship policies. This is the essence of political scientist James Rosenau's claim about the "fragmegration" — a mixture of fragmentation alongside integration — of authority in a messy world within which disaggregating old authority structures are being only partially integrated into new ones (Rosenau, 2003, p. 11).[7]

Third and finally, in navigating hybrid sovereignty, states need to work out how to operate across layers of governance, ranging from national to sub- to

---

[7] Rosenau, J. N. (2003). *Distant Proximities: Dynamics beyond Globalization*. Princeton, NJ: Princeton University Press, 2003.

trans- to supranational levels. That is, practising effective hybrid sovereignty is less about controlling the national arena of governance than about forging relationships, creating linkages, leveraging comparative advantages in expertise and capabilities, and exploiting interdependence.

TRAJECTORIES FOR SINGAPORE'S SOVEREIGNTY

In the light of these globalisation challenges facing hybrid sovereign states, what do the key future trajectories for Singapore look like? Here, I do not consider involuntary possibilities that would compromise or render conditional Singapore's sovereignty. Such possibilities may include any number of "known and unknown unknowns" and multicoloured "swans" such as invasion, civil war or natural disasters. Instead, I will concentrate on three voluntary scenarios and their different implications for Singapore's sovereignty: (1) merger, (2) integration and (3) "global state".

MERGER: FEDERAL SOVEREIGNTY

Merger with neighbouring states or political entities will mean Singapore becoming a state within a federal system. In this scenario, Singapore's sovereignty will become partial. In other words, it will retain authority over internal services but authority over defence and other elements of national policy will devolve upwards to the federal government. This is by no means an ahistorical trend — consider German reunification and the remaining drives for unification on the Korean peninsula and between elements of the Republic of China and the People's Republic of China. In Singapore's case, possible mergers would be with Malaysia (re-merger), Malaysia and Indonesia (in a broader Indo-Malayan federation) or some version of "Greater China".

The possible logic would include consolidating control over intensifying economic networks. This might be a logical outcome of an intensification of the so-called "region state", or economic zones with integrated industrial investment and information systems that already cross these national boundaries. Here, the growth of regional production networks spanning East Asia and the projected rise of the Asian consumer market as a leading global market are strong economic forces that will push in the direction of merger.[8]

---

[8] Linda Lim emphasises the importance of these regional economic factors in her chapter in this volume, although she does not discuss the prospects for merger.

However, very major obstacles remain in the form of political, ideological and historical divides as well as significant lags in the military capabilities and economic profiles between Singapore and its neighbours.

INTEGRATION: POOLED SOVEREIGNTY

Regional integration within ASEAN or a bigger East Asian union will entail Singapore "pooling" sovereignty with other union partners: transferring key authorities to a shared central governing institution, accepting porous borders and committing to greater institutional transparency. Again, integration is not an ahistorical prospect. The countries of Eastern and Central Europe, even the Caucasus, have been keen to join the European Union while some countries in the ex-Soviet sphere have been voluntarily trying to move towards reintegration with Russia on the security front.

The possible logic driving the integration impulse would be that pooling sovereignty would help to address the effectiveness and intervention challenges that other models cannot. For instance, ASEAN economic integration may provide the necessary joint resources, expertise and political oversight necessary to help member states achieve vital economic and financial regulatory reforms that have been out of the reach of many states because of problems with individual capacity and the norm against external interference. However, integration is at heart a political project, and the very significant obstacles here include lack of political will to overcome the basic principle of sovereign non-interference, something that is held particularly strongly by the post-colonial states in the region. At the same time, very wide regional gaps exist in vital areas of functional competence necessary for political union or economic integration, including legal and administrative capacities, and technical and financial expertise.

In considering the merger and integration futures, Singapore's leaders will have to ask: how would getting bigger and giving up elements of sovereign authority help to overcome globalisation's challenges? My sense is that fundamentally, Singapore — and the rest of its region — remains politically wedded to notions of sovereignty closer to the absolute end of the spectrum. For this reason, the next possibility is the most likely and best bet.

"GLOBAL STATE": HYPER-HYBRID SOVEREIGNTY

Singapore should aim to be an extraordinarily effective "global state" practising hyper-hybrid sovereignty. In some ways, this is a "more of the same, but more effectively" scenario. As discussed above, all states are subject to hybrid practices of sovereignty in the globalised era, whether they like it or not, and state effectiveness is more than ever before not a simple function of size. It is more likely to be related to the degree to which the state is plugged into global networks and flows (measured, for instance, by the trade index). Singapore as a classic trading state is closer to the more "plugged in" end of the spectrum.

Most states will be in limbo of the hybrid sovereignty that I have described above for the foreseeable future, and into the next 50 years. This is because there is probably no need or functional advantage to taking radical steps like merger or integration. The more important questions are: How can we manage the opposing forces of de- and renationalisation to maximise state capacity? How can we best leverage multiple systems of rule to achieve national purposes? How can we reconcile modern versus post-modern modes of sovereign practice in currently dichotomous realms (for instance, economics versus security, citizenship versus entrepreneurship and labour versus economy)?

In thinking through these vital questions, it is helpful to consider the key challenges Singapore faces across the security, economic and social realms as it strives to be a successful global state.

SECURITY

As indicated in the chapter by Ambassador Bilahari Kausikan, Singapore's national security realm will retain the most rigid notions of state sovereignty when it comes to defence planning, securing national borders and territory, conscription and deterrence. However, in spite of Singapore's considerable success in securing the vulnerable island state over the past 50 years, growing pressures and new challenges will arise with regard to defence relationships, international judicial authorities and security cooperation.

Singapore's successful national security strategy to date has been built on a combination of impressive autonomous defence capabilities and selective defence partnerships with major powers, especially the United States. Even though Singapore's Comprehensive Security Partnership with the US is not a formal alliance like those Washington has with Japan, South Korea or

Australia, Singapore is widely acknowledged to be the strongest US partner in Southeast Asia. In the years ahead, Singapore is likely to find the strengths and limits of this relationship put to the test by crises (for instance, conflict over territories or sea lanes of communication in the South China Sea) or if other rising powers like China decide to put more pressure on US security partners in the region to loosen their support for US primacy.

Beyond geostrategic competition though, Singapore will have to balance other considerations in its defence partnerships. For instance, to what extent do procurement, training and joint operability relationships with strategic partners make demands on Singapore's sovereign prerogatives? While these arrangements will vary depending upon the particular acquisition or context, the intensifying power political contest many expect to see between the US and China in the region may eventually exert external pressures akin to those of the Cold War upon these considerations. For example, in modifying and updating strategic and acquisition plans with future conflict contingencies in mind, Singapore defence planners are likely to have to put on the table a range of joint operability options with their US partners. These would span a spectrum including joint command (e.g., NATO) and/or subordinated command (e.g., South Korea within the ROK-US alliance), both of which would involve significant decisions to cede sovereign autonomy over the state's armed forces in combat. Another example is defence acquisitions from strategic partners. While Singapore has tended to take a pragmatic, often market-based, approach to purchasing foreign defence equipment, the US is its primary source for high-technology systems. But this is a double-edged sword — highest-end defence technology transfers ultimately depend upon the limits to national security determined by the seller's state (witness the constraints on US defence companies in selling its newer generation fighter jets, for instance). And while such sales might aid the development of the defence industry within the buyer's state, dependence on foreign technology might also limit domestic innovation and promote lower-end production.

Yet, security is not just about arms, alliances and deterrence. In the increasingly prominent realm of territorial conflicts, for instance, legal and other internationally agreed norms and rules of conduct can be just as important. In this regard, Singapore already acknowledges and uses multiple systems of authority beyond the sovereign state when it comes to territorial disputes. Notably, Singapore submitted its dispute with Malaysia over some small islands at the entrance to the Singapore Straits to the International Court of Justice, which ruled in 2008 that Singapore had sovereignty over Pedra Branca and Malaysia over Middle Rocks. The two sides were also eventually able to reach an out-of-court bilateral agreement after Malaysia submitted a complaint to the International Tribunal for the Law of the Sea in 2003 about the impacts of Singapore's land reclamation works in Tuas and Pulau Tekong on the Johor Straits waterway. In the decades ahead, Singapore should look to play a more active role in developing these international judicial authorities. In return for ceding some sovereign autonomy, states get a strengthened international legal system that undergirds the rule of law regulating international life.

We may confidently expect collective action demands in the security realm to grow, whether it relates to terrorism, piracy or the intertwined areas of territorial claims, juridical practice and resource development. Singapore can play an important role in leading, coordinating and shaping these cooperative enterprises, with creative and adaptive balancing between strengthening supranational rule of law and pooling or ceding certain sovereign rights in particular issue areas. For example, in the South China Sea conflicts, Singapore can take the lead by creating multiple, mutually-reinforcing levels of voluntary restraint and deterrence. These could include persuading ASEAN states to adopt a binding code of conduct amongst themselves as a first step towards a code of conduct that would include China and creating a regional system of pooling sovereignty for maritime security surveillance built upon a defence guarantee with the major maritime powers in the region.

ECONOMY

Because Singapore is a global trading state and financial hub, the economic realm is already the most globalised and networked. As discussed earlier, over the last five decades, the international political economy has spawned important actors, apart from the state, in the form of MNCs and multilayered governance regimes and institutions. Against this background, the challenges ahead are about maximising Singapore's weight and agility within the complex international political economy.

To understand the demand for agility, we need to return to my earlier observation that state authority has disaggregated upwards towards supranational institutions and downwards towards subnational or local actors, in the face of globalisation. But that is not the whole story. State authority has been reforming "sideways" as well. Component government institutions, regulatory agencies, ministries, courts and legislatures are increasingly interacting semi-autonomously with their foreign counterparts. As international lawyer and former Director of Policy Planning at the U.S. State Department Anne-Marie Slaughter argues, these state bodies and actors interact globally in a "networked" manner (Slaughter, 2004, pp. 283–327).[9] For instance, central banks and finance ministers of member states, standard-setting bodies (the Basel Committee on Banking Supervision, the International Accounting Standards Board, the International Organization of Securities Commissioners and the International Association of Insurance Supervisors) and international organisations (the Bank for International Settlements, IMF, the Organisation for Economic Cooperation and Development and the World Bank) work as a joint network through the Financial Stability Forum (FSF).[10] Moreover, within the FSF for example, bankruptcy judges from different states could negotiate what were effectively "mini treaties" in order to resolve complex international cases.

To be most effective at asserting and protecting its sovereignty, a state needs to maximise the depth and breadth of its connections to and engagement with these international networks of institutions. Singapore, despite its small size, has managed to participate in all of the key global financial networks that have evolved over the last two decades. For instance, it is a member of the International Monetary and Financial Committee (IMFC) of the IMF, which provides crucial strategic advice to the Fund's Board of Directors. It is also part of the Global Governance Group (3G), an informal grouping of 30 small- and medium-sized countries promoting greater transparency and inclusivity in the G20 process. Due to its 3G and IMFC activities, Singapore was invited to participate in the G20 summits in four out of the six years for which they have been held. Soon after the FSF was formed in 1999 by G7 financial officials to coordinate the emerging international monetary and financial standards process, the Monetary Authority of Singapore (alongside those of Australia and Hong Kong) was invited to become a member, and remains a member of the

---

[9] Slaughter, A. (2004). Sovereignty and Power in a Networked World, *Stanford Journal of International Law*, 40, 283–327.
[10] Restyled as the Financial Stability Board (FSB) in 2009.

expanded FSB that includes all G20 countries. Singapore needs to build upon its good record to leverage even more its connectivity and expertise not just in the realms of finance but also in trade, crime, terrorism and climate change. Rather than aiming narrowly to enhance its national autonomy, Singapore would better profit from getting a good seat in these transnational governance institutions that will become nodes of global governance. Ensuring that it continues to play a critical role in helping to make the emerging "rules of the game" in these vital realms, without necessarily engaging in enterprises to negotiate federal or pooled sovereignty, is one crucial way in which Singapore must cultivate "hyper-hybrid" sovereignty.

SOCIETY

This realm contains the most complex challenges because the potential trade-offs may be zero-sum as the state is required to face opposing pressures resulting from globalisation and reconcile dichotomous demands of sovereign practice. For instance, in the contest between preserving national identity and maintaining a sufficient labour force to support economic growth, Singapore society needs to adapt and absorb outsiders at a rate that keeps up with the economy's need for foreign labour. Government policies to facilitate this difficult balance may entail regulations that impact upon the domestic policy choices of other states, for example, if particular skill requirements were made vis-à-vis all foreign workers in the service sectors. Alternatively, it may result in revisions to core tenets of Singapore's national identity, for instance, the weakening of English as the working language or of the national policy of bilingualism.

Another conundrum is the growing divergence between citizenship and geography. How can the Singapore government leverage the talents of the Singapore diaspora without necessarily requiring them to be located on the island? Squaring this circle may entail changes to long-held policies such as the ban on dual nationality or to more recent policies such as restrictions on ownership of public housing for those who own private property abroad. A myriad of other challenges abound, amongst which is the question of how the civil service would cultivate "global" diplomats and other state actors while at the same time keep them grounded in the realities of Singapore's domestic socio-political economy? There are no easy answers to this question, which goes to the heart of the challenge posed by the intense era of globalisation that we have already entered.

CONCLUSION

It might have been more exciting if I could have presented three wild and wonderful alternatives to Singapore's future as a sovereign state that no one else has thought of, if only to spur us all to think "out of the box". However, we are not dealing with static practices that are coming under sudden and urgent threat now. Rather, globalisation as well as the institution of sovereignty are both trends that have been undergoing significant evolution, and state responses have already been evolving in tandem. Hence, it is important to map the big picture contours of this ongoing evolution and highlight the key questions that will become even more trenchant in the years to come as we live the reality of Singapore's future in a world of hybrid sovereignty. The future is not something that will begin at some point down the line; the future has already started.

2

Global City

3

Managing Singapore's Globalisation and Its Discontents: A Long-Term Perspective

TAN KONG YAM

INTRODUCTION

Globalisation has been an extremely powerful force that has impacted on the Singapore economy since its formation in 1965. Yet its effect has only been gathering momentum over the past four decades. This chapter attempts to examine the effect of globalisation and its discontents in Singapore. It then proposes a framework and strategy for managing globalisation — its relative winners and losers — so as to maintain long-term social stability. Lastly, it highlights a very important policy measure in the era of globalisation: the need to sustain the mothership for the Singapore economy.

Over the past decade, the real median wages for employed residents in Singapore has risen steadily. However, the low end has stagnated while the higher end has increased substantially (Figure 1). This rise in inequality has basically been a global phenomenon.

The same phenomenon can be observed in the United States. There, the same scenario has occurred, whereby the high income of educated people has risen while the real wages of high school graduates and dropouts have declined (Figure 2).

This phenomenon is independent and bears no relation to the effect of foreign worker inflow. Figure 3 shows the income ratio of the top 10% versus the bottom 10%. Clearly, income inequality has widened. As South Korea, unlike Singapore, is closed to the inflow of foreign workers, it indicates clearly the universal impact of globalisation on income inequality across countries.

Figure 1   Real median wages of employed residents, 1996–2012

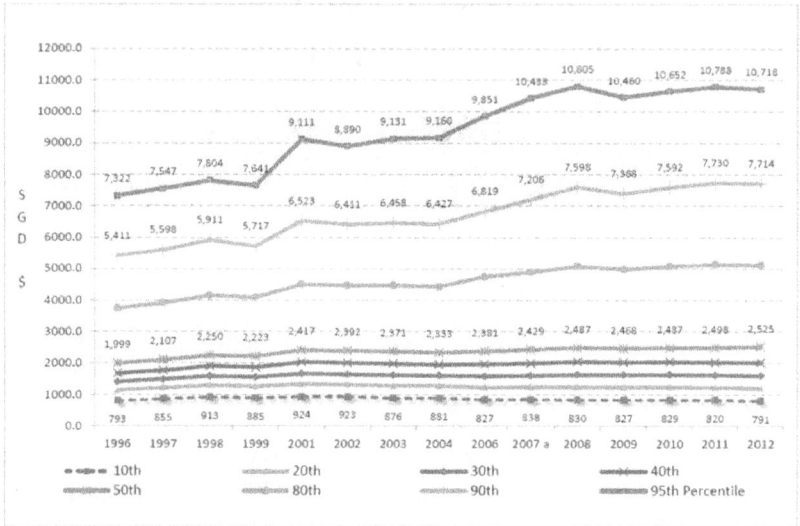

Source: Hui Weng Tat

Figure 2   Changes in wages for full-time, full-year male US workers, 1963–2008

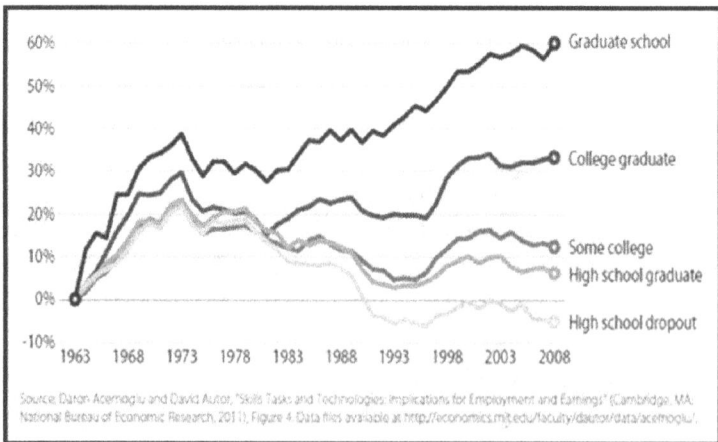

Figure 3 Rising income inequality in Korea

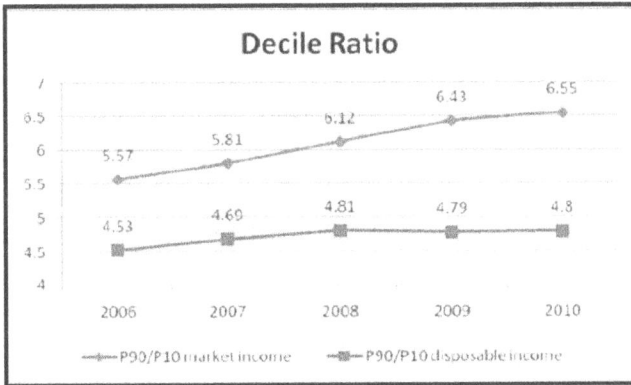

MANAGING GLOBALISATION AND ITS DISCONTENTS

Globalisation is inevitable and necessary for Singapore so that we can retain our long-term economic vibrancy. Had things been otherwise, with Singapore being mostly dependent on the domestic Malaysian hinterland for growth, what would have happened? The development of Penang serves as an illustration. In the mid-sixties, the port in Penang was almost as big as Singapore's port. Today, Singapore's port, which handled 580 million tonnes of cargo through 2013, is almost 20 times larger than Penang's port.

Consequently, we are in this globalisation race. Singapore is like a top. We need to spin with sufficiently strong angular momentum and ensure that we do not slow down too much. Otherwise the top will wobble. So what are the best management strategies to maintain long-term social stability? It can be argued that globalisation in the case of Singapore resulted in almost everybody being an absolute winner. But the key problem here is that we also care about relative winners and relative losers, not just absolute winners. So who are the relative winners? The government is a relative winner because it owns a lot of land. The other major relative winners are the domestic and global elites as well as capital in general. Who are the relative losers? The lowest 30% of the population has felt the competitive pressure of globalisation very keenly as well as some of the pressure from the inflow of foreign workers exerting downward pressure on real wages. Another group could include aspiring members of the middle class who want to buy cars and houses but are not able to take advantage of these opportunities because of land constraints.

Singapore has a unique problem because we are a global city as well as a small state. In order to sustain our global city status, we need to top up our talent pool. We have targeted and carefully managed the inflow of foreign skilled workers. Unfortunately, we are a city-state without any hinterland so there is no natural outflow of local people who are less competitive or have less drive. Due to this lack of land, they are not able to move to smaller towns, which are less stressful and cheaper to live in, as is possible in larger countries where, for instance, people can move from New York to Oklahoma or from Shanghai to Anhui. Consequently, we need to help these less competitive and less driven people trapped in a competitive global city.

The present tension between London and Scotland is illustrative. London is a global financial and talent capital. It wants to attract all the global talent and money to the city so, consequently, it wants a strong currency and does not mind escalating property prices and the rising cost of living. The local elites and capital are chief beneficiaries of this policy measure. However, the strong currency resulted in deindustrialisation in Scotland and we witnessed rising nationalism among Scots who have been considering independence.

Singapore is now experiencing similar tension. The Marina Bay Financial Centre and Shenton Way is our counterpart of London. Where is our Scotland? It is Hougang. The financial centre wants global talent and capital to come in and it also wants a strong Singapore dollar to maintain international confidence and capital inflows and sustain the wealth management industry. As a result, the strong Singapore dollar and rising costs of living are squeezing the small- and medium-sized enterprises (SMEs) in Hougang. However, Hougang cannot become independent and declare Teochew as its national language. So what can its inhabitants do? They can vote for the Workers' Party. Now if there were to become too many Hougangs, this spreading dissatisfaction could lead to greater potential for social political instability. Consequently, in order to avoid this from happening, we have to make sure that the centre takes care of the peripheries. That means the relative winners have to realise that they need to compensate the relative losers in order to sustain long-term socio-political stability before this tension intensifies. How can we achieve this and what is the monitoring mechanism? We are a small open economy. We are much like a balloon bobbing in a turbulent ocean. In my past incarnation, I was chief economist for the government so I am fully aware that it is not easy to sustain the stability of the Singapore economy in the midst of such volatility and turbulence. As indicated in Figure 4, the volatile external demand is 80% of total demand for the Singapore economy.

Moreover, if you look at volatility measures in terms of the standard deviation of Singapore's gross domestic product (GDP) cycle, the economy has been getting more volatile (Figure 5).

Figure 4 Domestic versus external demand

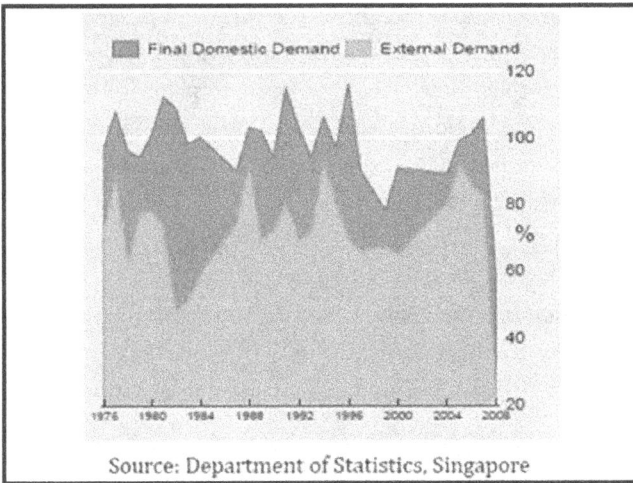

Source: Department of Statistics, Singapore

Figure 5 Singapore's GDP cycle when volatility has risen

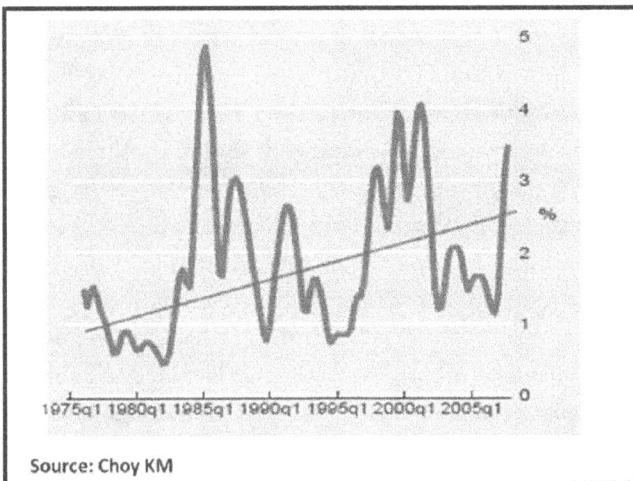

Source: Choy KM

Fortunately, there are strategies to address some of these problems. For example, while the balloon is bobbing in the turbulent ocean, you can tie a rock to the balloon and stabilise it. What could be the rock? First, the government should act as a collective risk insurer and diversifier as well as a social and political stabiliser. There is, for example, uncertainty in housing demand. The government should not pass the risk of uncertainty of housing demand to individual households; instead it should absorb it. So individually we might be a small sampan caught in the turbulent ocean but if collectively we raft it together into a more stable and (much larger) vessel through government policy, then things will become more stable for us in the turbulent ocean. Which key institutions could act as the rock? The Central Provident Fund is one risk insurer and diversifier while GIC, Temasek and the Monetary Authority of Singapore are others. In addition, I think that subsidies in education, healthcare, public transport and food (in terms of hawker rentals), especially for the lowest 30%, would be critical.

Before I consolidate the analysis into a framework for the stabilisation of Singapore's society in the turbulent world of globalisation, I would like to highlight several pertinent points. First, we have a Singapore premium. This brand premium is very valuable. What are the sources of this premium? Everybody knows that we have good governance, meritocracy, a clean government, multiracialism, openness, great infrastructure, security and robust institutions. This premium has been built up by generations of Singaporeans and the government and includes the national service obligation as well as the sacrifices of the pioneer generation. I did not realise how valuable the Singapore premium is until I worked abroad at the World Bank in Beijing between 2002 and 2005. While there, I was given US$6 million of research funds to manage even though I was relatively junior. I was made the chairman of the committee because they thought that it was safer to give the US$6 million to a Singaporean rather than to a Chinese, Indian or US citizen.

Now if you listen to the grouses on the ground, you see clearly that foreigners benefiting from this Singapore premium are one of them. Conceptually, foreigners who benefit from this premium, in a way, should be taxed and the benefits distributed to locals. It is like the McDonald's franchise. I build up this golden arches brand. If you then want to sell burgers under this brand name, you would have to pay me franchise fees. The only problem is that in the real world, it is much more complicated. Singapore is a price-taker.

If London and Hong Kong do not tax foreign skilled workers, can we afford to implement such a tax? If McDonald's does not ask for a franchise fee, can BreadTalk ask for a franchise fee?

FRAMEWORK AND STRATEGY FOR MANAGING GLOBALISATION

I would like to propose a conceptual framework for policymakers to monitor closely to ensure that the lower and middle classes are not squeezed. As indicated in Figure 6, median nominal monthly income, which is the 50th percentile income level every year in nominal terms, is plotted against the various costs of living. I indexed the year 2001 as 100. Then I looked at four key costs of living. The first key cost is food (Figure 6). You can see clearly in some years that income did not cover the price of food but, overall, the nominal income, even in the lowest 50%, has managed to cover food over 10 to 15 years. Consequently nominal income has been able to keep pace with food prices.

Figure 6　Food/median gross monthly income

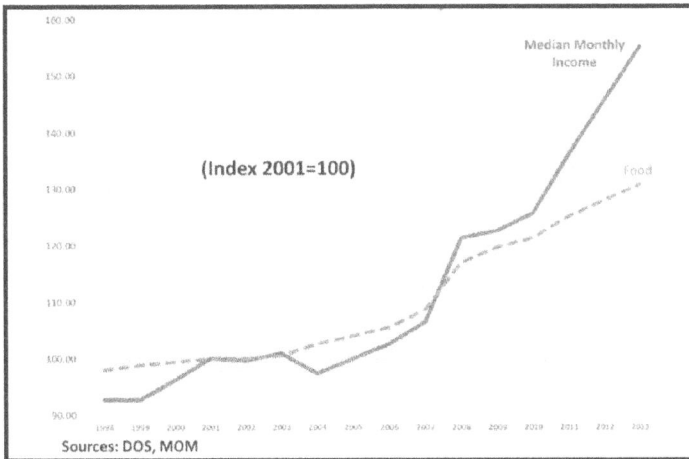

Then we look at transport (Figure 7). There were periods when public transport and private transport prices increased faster but, overall, the figures indicate that nominal income of the lowest 50th percentile could still manage to cover the transport price increases over the past decade.

43

Figure 7 Transport/median gross monthly income

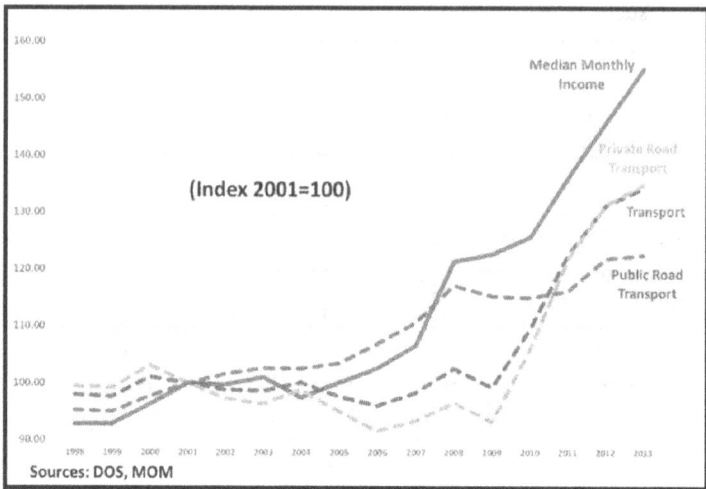

Figure 8 Healthcare/median gross monthly income

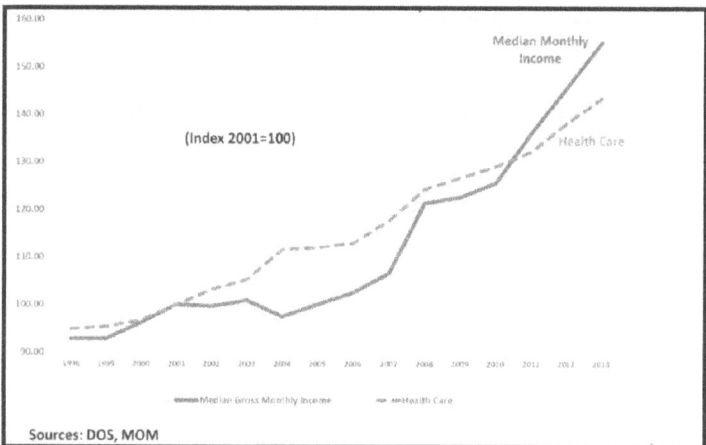

When we look at healthcare, the trend appears somewhat worrying (Figure 8). Clearly for quite a sustained period, from 2001 to 2010, healthcare costs increased much faster than the income of the lowest 50%. Recently it has improved, but this is an area in which we are likely to see flashing red lights in the future.

Housing appears to be the biggest problem (Figure 9). Not many people realised that after the Asian financial crisis, from 1998 to 2007, HDB resale prices remained flat or actually went down for almost a decade due to excess supply. However since 2007, HDB resale prices have increased greatly, even more than private property prices. In the last few years, it has increasingly overshot the median monthly income. In Figure 9, however, the line labelled "housing DOS" shows that it is lower than median income growth. This is because the Singapore Department of Statistics (DOS) housing price is computed according to the United Nations System of National Accounts. It shows imputed rental price and is probably not representative of the actual housing price effect on the population due to the small rental market in Singapore for public housing.

Figure 9 Housing/median gross monthly income

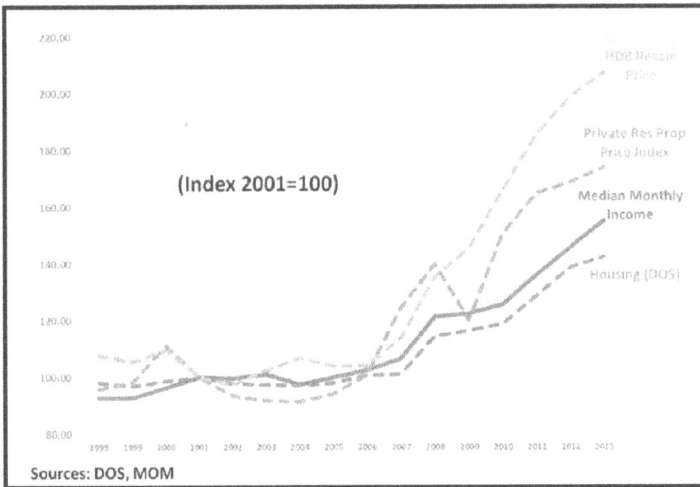

Figure 9 shows substantial overshooting of housing prices over nominal income growth. Fortunately, since 2011, credit tightening has enabled an increase in supply. More significantly, the Build-to-Order (BTO) price was delinked from the resale price. Consequently, in the four quarters of 2014, we began to see prices falling (Figure 10). It can be argued that public housing should be like utilities, and not an asset. Public housing prices should move roughly in line with nominal income. If public housing is an appreciating asset, much like Internet stock, then you have a situation in which the young new entrants are angry but, more importantly, almost everybody who owns an HDB flat will be unhappy. This is because every HDB owner is a potential upgrader. If HDB prices double and income does not double, an owner's ability to upgrade becomes much more difficult. Thus it affects everybody. I would argue that by looking at Figure 9, by 2009 alarm bells should have started to ring for the Housing and Development Board because resale prices had overshot 20% of the income line. Consequently, I would argue that this framework is useful in providing an early warning system to policy makers to ensure that the various costs of living do not go too far out of line with the nominal income of the lowest 50% of the population.

The analogy for this is taking annual blood tests. The results of the tests will show things like your liver function, full blood count sugar level and cholesterol level. These are benchmarked against a normal range so that if any of them goes beyond the normal range, you immediately know what the problem is and you try to address it before you suffer any major health issues or complications. This framework can also be refined for the lowest 10%, and if you are worried about the middle class, for the middle 60%.

Figure 10   Price index of HDB resale flats

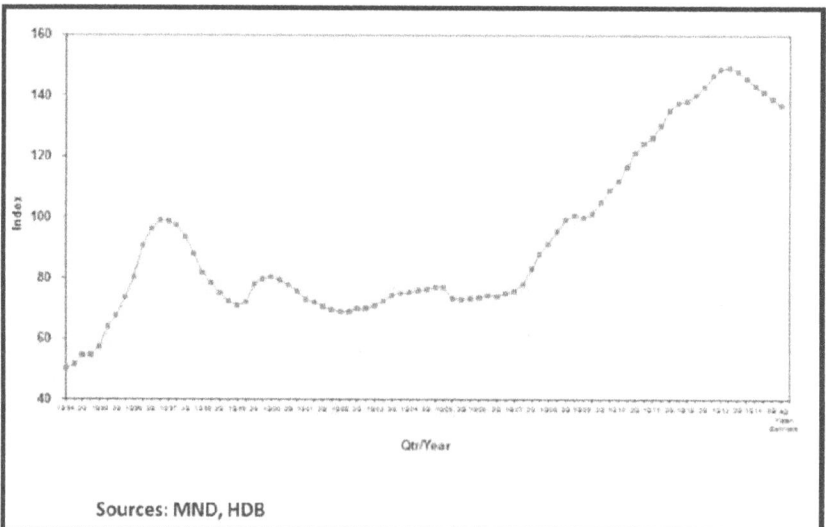

Sources: MND, HDB

It should also be noted that the government has effectively used public funds accumulated over the years. A good example of this is as follows. During the global financial crisis of 2008–09, the government spent S$4.5 billion on the job credit scheme, S$5.8 billion in special risk sharing to stimulate bank lending and a total package of S$20.5 billion to support the people and the economy (Figure 11). As a result, we ended with a big deficit (Figure 12).

Figure 11 Resilience package — The key components (in S$ billions)

Preserve jobs	5.1
- Jobs Credit Scheme	4.5
Stimulate bank lending	5.8
- Special Risk-Sharing Initiative	5.8
Enhance business cashflow and competitiveness	2.6
- Property tax rebate for commercial and industrial property	0.8
- Rental rebate for selected industrial and commercial tenants	0.3
Support families	2.6
- Personal income tax rebates	0.5
- Doubling GST credits and Senior Citizen Bonuses	0.5
Build for the future	4.4
- Expanded and accelerated infrastructure spending	1.1
- Spending on security, health, education, transport	1.7
Total package	20.5

Source: Budget 2009; MAS, *Macroeconomic Review* (April 2009).

Figure 12 Primary surplus/deficit

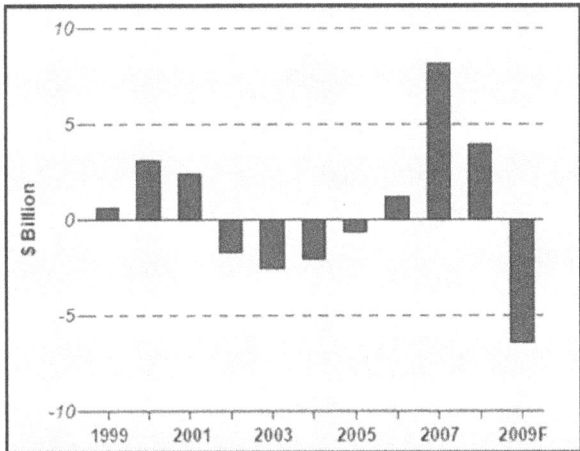

Figure 13 Total employment changes

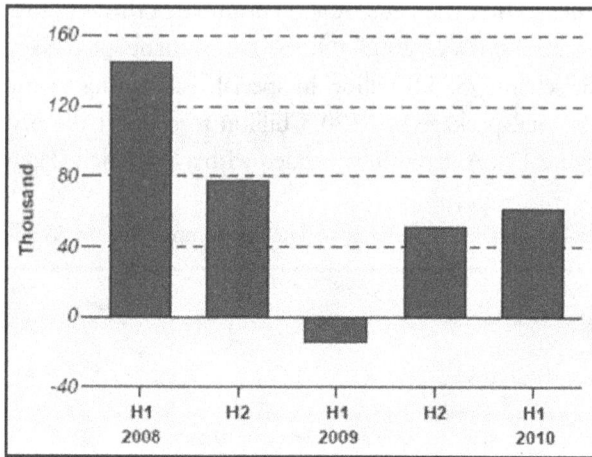

Figure 14 Employment growth since the start of the great recession by country

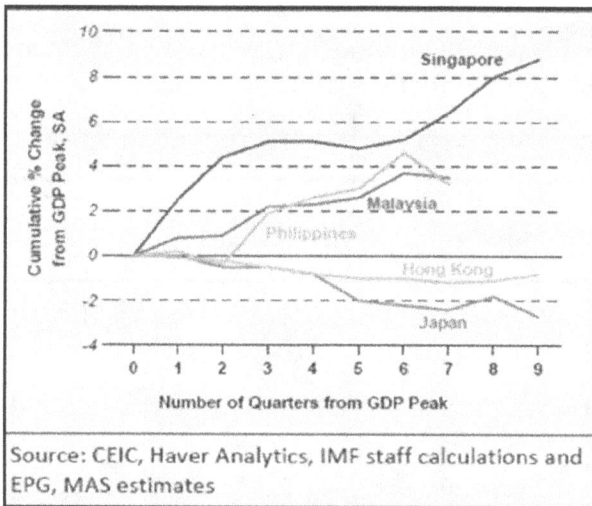

The advantage of taking such action was that employment did not decline very much during the financial crisis (Figure 13). If you look at the International Monetary Fund (IMF) analysis across the Asian countries (Figure 14), Singapore is the only country where employment growth recovered very quickly after the Asian financial crisis (Figure 14). So, in a way, public funds have been spent well and wisely to protect the population from serious global shocks.

SUSTAINING THE MOTHERSHIP

The powerful forces of globalisation can be overwhelming. I would now like to address the critical issue of sustaining the mothership. The Singapore brand premium is crucial and that is why we need to sustain the mothership. What do I mean by sustaining the mothership? Is it important in the era of globalisation? I want to compare Singapore to Taiwan and Hong Kong. The economies of Taiwan and Hong Kong are not doing well at the moment. Wages are stagnating, especially for young graduates (Figure 15). This is part of the reason for the discontent among young people in Hong Kong.

Taiwanese new graduates have suffered even more. Entry-level nominal wages for Taiwanese graduates in 2011 were actually lower than they were in 1997, even before accounting for rising inflation (Figure 16).

Wages may well be stagnating but Taiwanese and Hong Kong companies are doing very well. Companies' profits are huge and continue to increase for the likes of Foxconn, Acer, Uni-President, Li & Fung, Chow Tai Fook and property tycoons in Hong Kong. This is because globalisation allows companies and elites labour and capital to separate themselves from the mothership.

Figure 15 Stagnating wages — Hong Kong

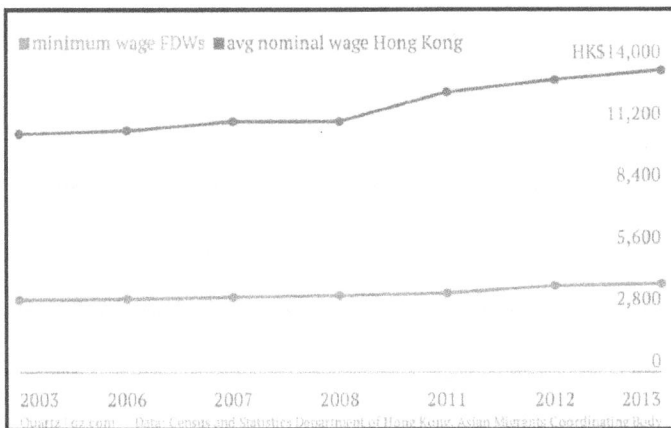

Figure 16 Taiwan: Stagnating entry-level wages of fresh graduates

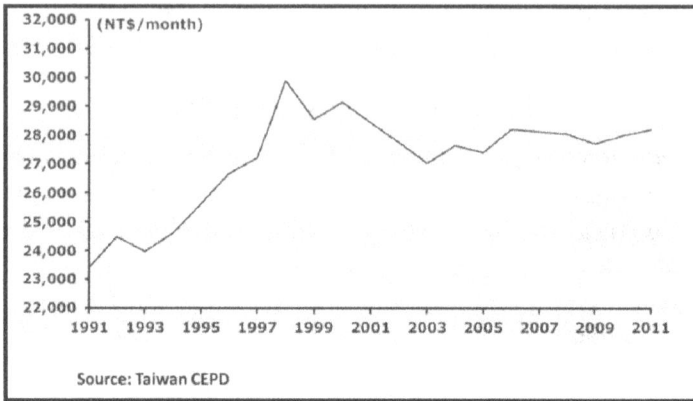

Source: Taiwan CEPD

It is well and fine to globalise and have a second wing. However, we have to protect our mothership because that is where our core is. It determines whether our people are getting good jobs or not. It determines whether our young new graduates see a future for themselves in this country. So while we encourage the development of the second wing, we have to make sure that the second wing does not cause the whole bird to fly away. That means that we have to work hard to strengthen the mothership and all the things that I mentioned earlier that make up the Singapore premium.

CONCLUSION

To conclude, I suggest we should monitor closely the nominal median income relative to the various costs of living, namely, housing, transport, food and healthcare, as a way to ensure that the fruits of globalisation are properly distributed. Having such an early warning system can help to ensure that we are alerted to any issues before it becomes too late to address them. We should focus on the welfare of the relative losers — the lowest 30% of the population and aspiring members of the middle class — before they want to declare "independence". In addition, the government should play its role as a collective risk insurer and diversifier as well as social and political stabiliser. We also need to strengthen our mothership to make sure globalisation does not create centrifugal forces that tear our economy and society apart.

CHAPTER 4

Beyond the "Global City" Paradigm

LINDA LIM

THE ECONOMY AT INDEPENDENCE

At independence in 1965, Singapore's economy remained heavily dependent on its colonial-era role as a regional entrepôt, or import-export hub, linking South-east Asia to world markets through the provision of port, transport, commercial and financial services as well as British military services, which constituted nearly a third of the gross domestic product (GDP). Though Singapore's per capita income was already Asia's second highest, after Japan, unemployment was 12% of the labour force.

A decade earlier, a World Bank mission to Malaya (including Singapore) had recommended that the two British colonial territories embark on import-substituting industrialisation for what became known after the merger in 1963 as a "Malaysian Common Market" (International Bank for Reconstruction and Development, 1955).[1] Political separation in 1965, and the circumstances under which it occurred, made this an unlikely, or at least difficult, prospect. At the same time, there was occasional social unrest at home and political turbulence abroad, including Indonesia's *Konfrontasi* against Malaysia, the war in Vietnam and the Cultural Revolution in China.

---

[1] International Bank for Reconstruction and Development. (1955). *The Economic Development of Malaya*. Baltimore, Maryland: Johns Hopkins Press.

THE POST-INDEPENDENCE DEVELOPMENT STRATEGY

Fortunately for Singapore, another promising development strategy had already emerged elsewhere in the developing world — that of labour-intensive manufacturing for export to world markets. Puerto Rico's "Operation Bootstrap" began as early as 1948, soon to be followed by the export of garments manufactured by Chinese industrialists who fled to Hong Kong after the communist takeover of China in 1949. In 1965, Mexico established its Border Industrialization Program, or *Maquiladora*, and in 1966 the Kaohsiung Export Processing Zone (EPZ) was inaugurated in Taiwan, followed by the Masan zone in South Korea in 1970 and multiple EPZs in Malaysia and the Philippines in the 1970s.

This development strategy fit with the theory of comparative advantage, which argues that countries should specialise in the production and export of items that intensively use their relatively abundant factors of production. High unemployment suggested that Singapore too might be competitive in relatively labour-intensive industries. But the strategy was driven not just by comparative advantage, or supply-side factors. Technological and public policy changes in developed countries also contributed to favourable demand-side conditions for labour-intensive manufactured exports from developing countries.

Most notable in trade policy was the institution of Items 806.30 (in 1956) and 807.00 (in 1963) of the US Tariff Schedules, which exempted US-origin value-added from import duty (U.S. Tariff Commission, 1970).[2] In the contrary case of textiles and garments, low-wage developing countries were so successful in displacing production in developed countries that the General Agreement on Tariffs and Trade (GATT, precursor of the World Trade Organization) imposed Multifibre Arrangement (MFA) quotas limiting exports from individual countries from 1974 to 2004. Fortunately, as a relatively early exporter, Singapore, like Hong Kong, retained textile quotas much larger than those awarded to lower-wage later entrants like Bangladesh, giving it a measure of protection that preserved competitiveness in this labour-intensive sector longer than market forces would allow. From 1975, Singapore

---

[2] U.S. Tariff Commission. (1970, September). *Economic Factors Affecting the Use of Items 807.00 and 806.30 of the Tariff Schedules of the United States.* Tariff Commission Publication 339, Washington, DC.

also benefited from the GATT/WTO's Generalised System of Preferences (GSP) for developing countries until, together with the other Asian newly industrialised countries (NICs) of Hong Kong, Taiwan and South Korea, it was "graduated" (ruled ineligible by income level) by the US, (1989), European Union (1997) and Japan (2000) (Ow-Taylor & Ow, 1991).[3]

Technological developments in the semiconductor and consumer electronics industries also enabled and encouraged subdivision and offshore sourcing of labour-intensive parts and components of the electronics value-chain by multinationals like Fairchild Semiconductor, Texas Instruments and Hitachi, a subject I examined in 1975–76 through field research in Singapore and Malaysia for my PhD dissertation (Lim, 1978).[4] The other industry that Singapore bet big and successfully on was the then-also-labour-intensive shipbuilding and repair, transforming the abandoned British naval base facilities into commercial shipyards run by new government-linked companies (GLCs) like Keppel and Sembawang.

Resource-based comparative advantage was not the sole reason why these labour-intensive export industries developed. Also key to Singapore's success here was the parallel development of complementary competitive advantages through strategic industrial and social policy that built on the country's already established economic assets of good geographical location, deep-water harbour, free trade and capital flows, and commercial and physical infrastructure.

---

[3] Ow-Taylor, C. H., & Ow, C. H. (1991). Graduation from U.S. GSP: The Case of Singapore. *Journal of Asian Economics*, 2(2), 285–299.

[4] Lim, L. Y. C. (1978). Multinational Firms and Manufacturing for Export in Less-Developed Countries: The Case of the Electronics Industry in Malaysia and Singapore (PhD dissertation in Economics). University of Michigan, Ann Arbor. See also Leontiades, J. (1971). International Sourcing in the Less-Developed Countries. *Columbia Journal of World Business*, 6(6), 19–26, Moxon, R. W. (July 1974). Offshore Production in Less-Developed Countries: A Case Study of Multinationality in the Electronics Industry. Bulletin, Nos. 98–99. New York University Graduate School of Business Administration, Institute of Finance and Reynis, L. A. (1976). The Proliferation of U.S. Firm Third World Sourcing in the Mid-to-Late 1960s: An Historical and Empirical Study of the Factors Which Occasioned the Location of Production for the U.S. Market Abroad (PhD dissertation in Economics). University of Michigan, Ann Arbor.

Industrial policy measures undertaken by new state institutions (primarily the Economic Development Board, or EDB, founded in 1961) consisted mainly of a streamlined bureaucracy (then called a "one-stop shop" for investors), the provision of infrastructure such as subsidised industrial estates (e.g., Jurong Town Corporation, or JTC) and industrial financing (Development Bank of Singapore, or DBS), and various tax incentives, including one to explicitly encourage manufacturing for export, that were introduced in 1967.[5] Taiwan and Korea had similar policies but Singapore's were distinctive in two ways.

First, they focused largely on promoting inward foreign direct investment whereas policies in the other NICs privileged domestic private enterprises, which soon came to dominate their export manufacturing sectors. Second, Singapore integrated social policies into industrial development to a much greater extent than in other locations. Its signature social policy — "public" housing (Housing Development Board or HDB flats) that residents paid for through their own "forced savings" (in the Central Provident Fund, or CPF) — co-located labour-intensive factories, including the then iconic "flatted factories", with HDB residential high-rises. This facilitated employers' access to workers, especially young females who made up the vast majority of workers in textiles and electronics factories and typically worked around the clock (requiring rotating shifts). It also helped maintain low labour costs by reducing workers' costs of housing (due to a combination of scale economies and state subsidies) and transportation. At the same time, large state investments in healthcare and education raised labour productivity, and in education also provided vocational and technical training for specific manufacturing industries (Lim, 1989).[6]

---

[5] Singapore's industrial policies during the first two decades of independence have been extensively discussed in many studies, including Pang, E. F., & Lim, L. (1986). *Trade, Employment and Industrialisation in Singapore*. Geneva: International Labour Office and Chia, S. Y. (1989). The Character and Progress of Industrialization. In K. S. Sandhu and P. Wheatley (Eds.), *Management of Success: The Moulding of Modern Singapore* (pp. 250–279). Singapore: Institute of Southeast Asian Studies.

[6] Lim, L. Y. C. (1989). Social Welfare. In K. S. Sandhu and P. Wheatley (Eds.), *Management of Success: The Moulding of Modern Singapore* (pp. 171–197). Singapore: Institute of Southeast Asian Studies.

Political stability and labour peace were necessary to encourage investment because they ensured that export manufacturing for distant global markets, especially in short product life cycle industries like fashion garments and electronics, would not be disrupted by political upheaval or labour unrest. Notably, among the other NICs, Taiwan and Korea were under military rule with strict labour controls until democratisation in the late 1980s while Hong Kong was a British colony, all throughout the period of labour-intensive export manufacturing. Unlike these NICs, Singapore was nominally a parliamentary democracy, albeit one that had seen the left-wing political opposition eviscerated in the early 1960s, resulting in a one- or dominant-party government by the People's Action Party (PAP) that helped ensure political stability (Chan, 1989).[7] On the labour front, the PAP's control of the labour movement (National Trades Union Congress, or NTUC) and legislation restricting labour organisation and action (particularly the 1968 Employment Act) ensured that there were virtually no incidents of significant labour unrest over the next four decades (Raj, 1989).[8]

Thus both market forces (comparative advantage) and domestic government policies (creating competitive advantage) made Singapore's new export manufacturing industries competitive in a fortunately favourable global market context. At the same time, the focus on foreign investment linked its economy closely to the developed home markets of multinational employers. Between 1965 and 1973, just before Singapore suffered its first globally-induced recession as an independent nation, manufacturing value-added grew by 23.2% per year at current factor cost and 18.1% at 1968 constant prices while its share of GDP rose from 15% to 23% and the share of manufacturing output exported rose from 27% to 54%, and to 63% by 1985 (Chia, 1989, pp. 253–256).[9] By then, less than a decade after independence, the combination of very rapid labour-intensive growth and Singapore's small

---

[7] Chan, H. C. (1989). The PAP and the Structuring of the Political System. In K. S. Sandhu and P. Wheatley (Eds.), *Management of Success: The Moulding of Modern Singapore* (pp. 70–89). Singapore: Institute of Southeast Asian Studies.

[8] Raj, V. (1989). Trade Unions. In K. S. Sandhu and P. Wheatley (Eds.), *Management of Success: The Moulding of Modern Singapore* (pp. 144–197). Singapore: Institute of Southeast Asian Studies.

[9] Chia, 1989, op. cit.

labour force meant that "surplus labour" had been absorbed, full employment had been reached and labour shortages appeared, indicating a shift in comparative advantage.

Yet the initial policy response was to seek to maintain GDP growth and preserve the eroding competitiveness of labour-intensive activities by holding down wages through the institution of a tripartite National Wages Council (NWC) in 1972 and importing low-wage foreign labour. It was not until 1979 that a "second industrial revolution" was launched, with the goal of moving into higher-value industries, increasing productivity and wages, and reducing reliance on low-skilled and foreign labour. It was recognised that:

> *The economic success of the 1970s was, in retrospect, achieved not so much because of improvements in labour productivity but as a result of the influx of foreign labour and the increased numbers of women joining the labour force...*

> *... the availability of cheap low-skilled workers allowed many employers to continue with inefficient operations, thus threatening to defeat the national plan to move up the technological ladder.*

> *In line with the wage-correction policy introduced in 1979 to help employers automate their operations, the government decided to phase out all foreign workers and have a wholly Singaporean work-force by 1991... A foreign worker levy ... was introduced in 1982... in order to deter employers from becoming overly dependent on them.*[10] (Pang et al., 1989, p. 134)

THE "SECOND INDUSTRIAL REVOLUTION" AND AFTER

One of the downsides of being a "global city" hitched to the wagon of multinationals based in distant foreign markets is vulnerability to economic shocks in those markets. The externally driven recession that Singapore suffered in 1974–75 was partly responsible for the delay of policymakers to

---

[10] Pang, E. F., Tan, C. H., & Cheng, S. M. (1989). The Management of People. In K. S. Sandhu and P. Wheatley (Eds.), *Management of Success: The Moulding of Modern Singapore* (pp. 128–143). Singapore: Institute of Southeast Asian Studies. See also Pang, E. F., & Lim, L. (1982, Fall). Foreign Labour and Economic Development in Singapore. *International Migration Review, 16*(4), 548–576.

adjust to the loss of comparative advantage in labour-intensive manufacturing. Another severe recession in 1984–85 led to hesitation in following through the "Second Industrial Revolution", as its high-wage policy was blamed for the severity, though it was not the cause, of the recession.

> *In the 1970s, a low-wage policy encouraged labour-intensive activities, thus negating attempts to achieve high productivity. In the 1980s, wage increases were to be tied to productivity, but instead the high increases recommended across the board did not reflect inter-industry differences in productivity growth. In most cases, wage increases exceeded productivity and pushed labour costs beyond internationally competitive levels.*[11] (Pang et al., 1989, as cited in Pang & Lim, 1989, p. 136)

Dependence on foreign manufacturing investment for which there was growing international competition arguably also reduced the degrees of freedom that Singapore's policymakers had in adjusting to declining competitiveness. In retrospect, they appear to have responded in two ways: first, by seeking to change the factor endowments that underlie comparative advantage, specifically by relaxing immigration rules for highly educated or skilled professionals (Pang et al., 1989, p. 134)[12]; second, by continuing to add location-specific competitive advantages that would particularly appeal to capital- and skill-intensive industries, primarily infrastructure and investment incentives targeted to specific industrial "clusters". These policies reflect the

---

[11] See also Pang, E. F., & Lim, L. (1989). Wage Policy in Singapore. In *Government Wage Policy Formulation in Less-Developed Countries: Seven Country Studies* (pp. 75–101). Geneva: International Labour Office. Other relevant studies include Rodan, G. (1985). *Singapore's Second Industrial Revolution: State Intervention and Foreign Investment.* ASEAN-Australia Joint Research Project, Rodan, G. (1987). The Rise and Fall of Singapore's 'Second Industrial Revolution'. In R. Robison, K. Hewison and Richard Higgot (Eds.), *Southeast Asia in the 1980s: the Politics of Economic Crisis* (pp. 149–176). Sydney, Australia: Allen and Unwin and Leggett, C. (1994). Labour and Singapore's Second Industrial Revolution. In S. Jackson (Ed.). *Contemporary Development in Asian Industrial Relations* (pp. 77–97). Sydney, Australia: University of New South Wales Studies in Human Resource Management and Industrial Relations in Asia.

[12] Pang & Lim et al. (1989), op. cit., p. 134.

view of Professor Michael Porter (1990)[13] who states that a nation can escape the limitations of its factor endowments like land, natural resources, labour and the size of the local population by creating "new advanced factor endowments", such as skilled labour, a strong technology and knowledge base, government support and culture.

The policies were successful in maintaining and even growing manufacturing's share of GDP, which went from 22% in 1985 to 26% in 1990, where it remained through 2005 (Choy, 2010, p. 129).[14] This was in striking contrast to the sharp (roughly 50%) share drop in all other developed economies, except Korea, and the virtual disappearance of manufacturing in Hong Kong (Perry, 2012)[15], as predicted by the Fisher-Clark hypothesis that demand for, and employment in, services rises with income over time. The share of high-value-added (capital-intensive) sectors also increased, as reflected in the decline in manufacturing's share of employment from 26% in 1990 to 17% in 2005, and the "steady migration of industrial production over the last twenty years into technologically advanced and skill-intensive clusters, in particular electronics, petrochemicals, specialty chemicals and pharmaceuticals" (Choy, 2010, p. 131).[16]

However, this policy-induced move up the manufacturing value-added ladder was accompanied by a more concentrated industrial structure, heavily reliant on an electronics and, more recently, pharmaceutical cluster, both of which transmitted their highly volatile business cycles to Singapore's own GDP growth (Choy, 2010, p. 131).[17] In addition, studies have shown that in all stages of Singapore's industrial development — from the labour-intensive

---

[13] Porter, M. E. (1990). *The Competitive Advantage of Nations.* New York, NY: The Free Press.

[14] Choy, K. M. (2010). Singapore's Changing Economic Model. In T. Chong (Ed.), *Management of Success: Singapore Revisited* (pp. 124–138). Singapore: Institute of Southeast Asian Studies.

[15] Perry, M. J. (2012, March 22). Manufacturing's Declining Share of GDP is a Global Phenomenon, and It's Something to Celebrate. US Chamber of Commerce Foundation. Retrieved from http://www.uschamberfoundation.org/blog/post/manufacturing-s-declining-share-gdp-global-phenomenon-and-it-s-something-celebrate/34261.

[16] Choy, op. cit.

[17] Ibid.

1970s to the capital- and skill-intensive 2000s — productivity growth has been weak to non-existent.[18] This most likely reflects the input-intensive nature of Singapore's growth, which has been achieved by adding mostly foreign capital, skills and labour to production rather than by increasing the productivity of domestic factors of production. As an example, a recent international innovation index ranked Singapore No. 1 in "Overall Innovation Input" each year from 2011 to 2014, but only No. 17 in "Overall Innovation Output" in 2011, declining to No. 25 in 2014, and No. 94 in "Innovation Efficiency" in 2011, declining to No. 110 in 2014 (INSEAD 2015).[19] Other studies have attributed Singapore's high inequality, stagnant median wages, low wage-to-income and low consumption-to-GDP ratios and comparatively weak performance on "well-being" indices to this input-intensive growth model

---

[18] See, for example, Lee, T. Y. (1985). Growth without productivity: Singapore manufacturing in the 1970s. *Journal of Development Economics, 19*, pp. 25–38; Young, A. (1992). A Tale of Two Cities: Factor Accumulation and Technical Change in Hong Kong and Singapore. In O.J. Blanchard and S. Fischer (Eds.), *NBER Macroeconomics Annual 1992*. MIT Press; Young, A. (1995). The Tyranny of Numbers: Confronting the Statistical Realities of the East Asian Growth Experience. *Quarterly Journal of Economics, 110*, 641–80; Krugman, P. (1994). The Myth of Asia's Miracle. *Foreign Affairs* 73/6, 62–79; Chuang, P. M. (2009, March 23). S'pore scores low in labour productivity. *The Business Times*, citing a comparative study of 17 developed economies by the U.S. Department of Labor; and Nomura, K., & Amano, T. (2012, September). Labor Productivity and Quality Change in Singapore: Achievements in 1974–2011 and Prospects for the Next Two Decades, KEO Discussion Paper No. 129, Keio Economic Observatory, Keio University. The most detailed and excellent analysis of Singapore's productivity policies and performance since independence can be found in a three-part case from the Lee Kuan Yew School of Public Policy, *Singapore's Productivity Challenge*, Parts I, II and III, prepared by Hawyee Auyong under the supervision of Donald Low. Auyong, H. (2014). Singapore's Productivity Challenge, Parts I–III. Case Study Unit. Singapore: Lee Kuan Yew School of Public Policy. Auyong's analysis shows that economic planners expressed concerns about excessive dependence on foreign capital and labour, the limits of the export manufacturing model and their depressing impact on productivity growth from very soon after independence, and continuing to the present day.

[19] INSEAD (2015), *INSEAD Global Innovation Index*. Retrieved from: https://www. globalinnovationindex.org/content.aspx?page=past-reports.

(Lim, 2014).[20] Professor Tan Kong Yam's contribution to this volume explicitly links social discontent to the fact that "the bottom 30% and some of the aspiring members of the middle class" have lost out from globalisation while the government, local and global elites, and owners of capital have benefited.[21]

SINGAPORE'S ECONOMIC MODEL AT 50: A LOOK BACK

Becoming a "global city", and specifically a "node" in the evolving global supply chains of multinationals, was the best and probably only path to economic development that Singapore could have followed fifty years ago. It succeeded because external global forces, including multilateral trade liberalisation and the information and communications technology revolution, and internal domestic policies and outcomes were conducive. Comparative and competitive advantage together created the international competitiveness that enabled Singapore to develop a successful export manufacturing sector within a few years of independence. But comparative and competitive advantages are dynamic, and Singapore's small size and high growth meant that shifts in international competitiveness happened very rapidly, with comparative advantage in labour-intensive activities yielding quickly to skill- and capital-intensity.

Singapore's policymakers recognised all of the limitations and weaknesses of its economic model as they emerged. The Ministry of Trade and Industry reviewed the model and recommended new policies in 1986 (after the 1984–85 recession), 1991 (after a 1990 downturn), 1998 (after the 1997–98 Asian financial crisis), 2003 (after the tech bubble burst, the September 2011 terrorist attacks in New York and the SARS crisis) and 2010 (after the 2008 global financial crisis) (MTI 1986; 1991; 1998; 2003; 2010).[22] All the reports

---

[20] Lim, L. Y. C. (2014). After the Miracle: Singapore's Success. In R. E. Looney (Ed.), *Handbook of Emerging Economies* (pp. 202–226). London: Routledge.

[21] Please see the chapter by Professor Tan Kong Yam in this volume.

[22] Ministry of Trade and Industry, Singapore (MTI). (1986). *The Singapore Economy: New Directions*, Report of the Economic Committee; MTI. (1991). *Strategic Economic Plan: Toward a Developed Nation;* MTI. (1998) *Committee on Singapore's Competitiveness Report*; MTI. (2003) *Economic Review Committee*; MTI. (2010). *Economic Strategies Committee.*

emphasised the need to increase productivity[23] and move into higher value-added activities, though the actual sectors prioritised changed over time (to eventually include a cumulatively broad slate of industries and services). All assumed a continued global role for Singapore in multinational networks, and a leading role for government in the "restructuring" or "transformation" of the economy. Until the 2010 committee report, all featured a continued major role for manufacturing, referred to in 2003, as in 1986, as one of "the twin engines of manufacturing and services". And despite the earlier (1979) stated intention to reduce dependence on foreign labour, all reports emphasised the need for continued, if reduced, imports of foreign labour and, especially, foreign talent. To varying degrees, they also mentioned the need to develop domestic private entrepreneurship, recognised as a deficiency of the Singapore model compared with those of Hong Kong, Taiwan and South Korea.

Interestingly, relatively early on, as well as recently, Singaporean economists, myself included, voiced scepticism about high-tech manufacturing as a durable and desirable development strategy for Singapore in the long term, as these representative remarks show:

> *The question may be raised as to whether the government should be creating an artificial comparative advantage for Singapore in high-technology manufacturing, and indeed, whether it can succeed in doing so. The new strategy requires, apart from the foreign capital, technology and markets that Singapore's labor-intensive export manufacturing sector is already dependent on, increasing dependence on foreign skilled labor and expertise.*[24]
> (Lim, June 1983, p. 758)[25]

> *It is not apparent that Singapore has a comparative advantage in high-tech industry, at least in the short term. The prerequisites for success in high-tech industries are an abundance of scientific skills, large expenditure on R&D, and the availability of venture capital*

---

[23] For details, see Auyong (2014) op. cit.
[24] This paper refers to alternative development strategies discussed in Pang, E. F., & Lim, L. (1982). Political economy of a city-state. In *Singapore Business Yearbook*, 7–33. Research Collection Lee Kong Chian School of Business.
[25] Lim, L. Y. C. (June 1983). Singapore's Success: The Myth of the Free Market Economy. *Asian Survey, 26*(6), 752–764

and dynamic entrepreneurship.... Although much has been spent on technical, scientific, and engineering education and training in the past decade so that the talent pool is growing, it lacks experience and critical mass, and is expensive in comparison with that available in the other NICs, and even in some advanced countries.... Singapore does not have a ready availability of venture capital, in spite of its very high savings rate and its well-developed financial markets. (Chia, 1989, p. 274)[26]

In manufacturing, though, the planners are banking heavily on the biomedical industry... to spearhead industrial upgrading. Unfortunately ... biomedical output tends to be as volatile as electronics exports, being constantly subject to unpredictable demand fluctuations and changes in product mixes. Furthermore, the government is taking a calculated gamble in picking this industry as a putative winner. It is well known that the huge R&D investments in biotechnology have long gestation periods before basic research can be applied to the commercial production of new drugs and medical technologies, not to mention stiff competition in this area from other countries such as Korea, which arguably has a comparative advantage over Singapore. (Choy, 2010, p. 136)[27]

Reservations were also voiced about the continued dependence on both foreign and state enterprises

Secondly, the dominance of foreign enterprises and the public sector have to some extent crowded out domestic private enterprise. Foreign-owned enterprises and state-owned enterprises compete with domestic private enterprises in both the product and factor markets....

The crowding-out effect is likely to be more serious in the labour market, as foreign investors and the public sector compete for scarce skills, and cream off the best talents by offering attractive salaries and career perks, thus inducing an upward pressure on salaries. The ready availability of remunerative jobs in government and MNCs, continuing full employment, and rising wages tend to discourage entrepreneurial risk-taking among the younger generation.

---

[26] Chia, (1989), op. cit.
[27] Choy, (2010), op. cit.

The crowding-out effect also operates with regard to access to capital. The high contribution rates for employees set by the Central Provident Fund (CPF) have reduced personal disposable incomes and voluntary savings, and thus contributed to a scarcity of personal and household venture and risk capital....

Thirdly, the rising cost of doing business also penalizes domestic entrepreneurs in SMEs. Large-scale urban redevelopment, for instance, has led to serious dislocations of many small businesses ... as relocated businesses often face higher rentals in their new premises. Rising labour and utility costs, compliance with ... business regulations, have also impinged harder on the SMEs.

Fourthly, the tax system is biased against local entrepreneurs in manufacturing activities. The high tax rate on corporate profits and the absence of taxes on capital gains and windfall incomes have distorted entrepreneurial returns, thereby diverting entrepreneurial energies away from industrial production, which is characterized by long gestation periods, towards speculative activities in real estate and the stock market. And while the government offers wide-ranging tax incentives to promote industrial investments, local SMEs tend to benefit less than foreign MNCs because of the selection criteria.

Finally, social attitudes have bred risk aversion rather than the entrepreneurial spirit. This is the result of a paternalistic government, a strong regulatory environment, an emphasis on social conformity, an educational system emphasizing scholarship rather than creativity and innovativeness, and a growing intolerance of failure. (Chia, 1989, pp. 265–266[28])

and about the dependence on foreign workers:

The question we must answer sooner or later is this, 'When do we stop growing?'... at what point do we stop importing foreign workers and cease to encourage foreign entrepreneurs and capital in Singapore? Because of our limited land area, industrial expansion, together with the concomitant population expansion,

---

[28] Chia, (1989), op. cit.

will produce overcrowding to increasingly uncomfortable limits.
(Goh Keng Swee, as cited in Teh, 2014)[29]

[Given official projections of annual economic and productivity growth rates] … the population of foreign workers, temporary and permanent, will rise in Singapore in the 1980s. The benefits of such workers to the local economy are well known, but the potential social and economic costs they pose have yet to be closely examined. These include the costs of providing housing, public transportation, social services and recreational facilities.

… These costs will spill over to the local population, who will have to compete with the foreigners for scarce and increasingly costly housing, and for services such as transportation, recreation and public health facilities. Costs will escalate rapidly and Singaporeans may have to subsidize the increased services to accommodate the foreigners. Their dissatisfaction with the declining quality of life may lead to hostility against foreigners.

… These social problems will intensify as the composition of the foreign labor force becomes increasingly weighted toward workers from countries other than Malaysia…. As the nontraditional sources of labor increase, so will ethnic, cultural and linguistic differences, which may limit productivity as well as intensify problems of social cohesion and integration.

… The short-term flexibility foreign workers offer must be weighed against the need for a restructuring of the economy.
(Pang & Lim, 1981)[30]

To avoid an overdependence on imported labour, however, the government ought to review its policy on the intake of low-skilled foreign workers. By augmenting the size of the labour force, these migrant workers have held down economy-wide wage increase. But the same workers depress earnings at the lower end of the nominal wage scale because of their low productivity, thus

---

[29] Teh, K. P. (2014). Globalisation and Singapore's Discontent, talk given at the Asia Pacific Real Estate Association (APREA) Chairman/CEO Series, September 5.
[30] Pang, E. F., & Lim, L. (1981, August 4). Singapore's Foreign Workers: Are They Worth the Costs? *Asian Wall Street Journal.*

impacting on income distribution adversely. Worse, relying on them indefinitely implies that Singapore's economic progress would still be achieved primarily by increases in labour inputs rather than productivity improvements. Since there are upper limits to immigration and the population size, sustainable growth in the long run can only come from the latter. Hence, a slower pace of economic growth might not be a bad thing if it is achieved through productivity gains and is accompanied by less macroeconomic volatility. (Choy, 2010, p. 135)[31]

These consistent analyses reflect traditional economics, which is the "science" of the allocation of scarce resources among competing alternative uses. As I have explained elsewhere:

Comparative and competitive advantage both allow for government policy to influence a location's competitiveness in particular sectors, through selective investments that shape resource endowments, and tax incentives and subsidies to target resource allocation toward particular sectors.

However, these policies can be imitated with relative ease, leading to "beggar-my-neighbour" outcomes and excess capacity....

As a national economy moves up the technology ladder, the capital and opportunity cost of further state-directed shifts in comparative or competitive advantage escalates, given diminishing returns. Further, competition created by government policy rather than market forces introduces a large element of political risk into business decisions, encourages inefficiency in the allocation of resources, and reduces world welfare.

... These time-tested economic maxims boil down to one prognosis for Singapore's economic model—you can't have everything, even without size and resource constraints. Trying to achieve comparative advantages in too many sectors at once will only push up resource costs, aggravate negative externalities such as inflation and environmental degradation, and result in reduced competitiveness overall. Competitive advantage based on economies of scale, first-

---

[31] Choy, (2010), op. cit.

comer and agglomeration or cluster advantages derived from government policy rather than geographical advantages, are probably unsustainable. (Lim, 2009)

Singapore itself likely suffered recently from a "beggar-my-neighbour" event when Broadcom, a large US fabless semiconductor firm, announced that it was moving some of its operations out of Singapore to Ireland, leading to speculation that this could be due to the expiry of tax incentives.

Tax incentives reduced Broadcom's Singapore taxes by US$423 million (S$528 million) last year, and by US$399 million in 2012 — significant sums given that its net earnings were US$424 million last year and US$719 million in 2012...

[The company's annual report] said tax incentives such as those it enjoyed in Singapore "often require us to meet specified employment and investment criteria" in the relevant jurisdictions.

It added: "In a period of tight manufacturing capacity, our ability to meet Singapore content requirements in our products may be more limited, which may have adverse tax consequences".

Broadcom's decision to use its Irish trading company for some foreign operations was expected to "result in a similar foreign tax provision as our current Singapore tax incentive", it said. ("Clarity needed on whether chip dip a cause for worry", 2014)[32]

SINGAPORE'S ECONOMIC PROSPECTS: THE NEXT 50 YEARS

Singapore's "global city" economic model, successful in terms of delivering rising incomes and living standards for its citizens through high GDP growth in the first decades of independence, has recently come up against domestic resource and social constraints:

Singapore's continued policy of importing foreign capital, foreign labour, and foreign technology, and privileging foreign/global companies, to serve foreign markets, poses obvious local political, social, and cultural challenges for the nation and the state....

---

[32] Chia, Y. M. (2014, September 2). Clarity needed on whether chip dip a cause for worry. *The Straits Times*. Retrieved from http://www.straitstimes.com/st/print/2792236.

These policies, together with changes in the global economic environment and the globalization processes of multinational companies, have resulted in much more ambiguous impacts on the local population. GDP growth, hinged to globalization in specific ways dictated by the state, has in the past decade suffered multiple setbacks that reflect continued if not increased vulnerability to the vicissitudes of volatile regional and global economies.... The growth which has occurred has seen low shares in GDP for labour incomes (relative to capital returns), and consumption (relative to investments and government expenditures), increased income inequality, and a decline in the relative incomes of local Singaporeans relative to foreigners. The specific forms and requirements of GDP growth have also contributed to the undermining of national identity and social cohesion which previously held together the people of this "hub economy" and sustained their support for their government. (Lim & Lee, 2010, pp. 153–4)[33]

A great deal of policy and public interest has been devoted to these issues since the general election of 2011, in which opposition political parties made unprecedented gains in popular votes and parliamentary seats (Low & Vadaketh, 2014).[34] This suggests that the industrial and social policies so critical to past success have been found wanting in the current stage of development.

The PAP government has responded by working to improve housing affordability, reduce inflation and transport congestion, expand healthcare and social safety net provisions for the elderly and the lowest-income. It is also slowing (but not stopping) the inflow of foreign workers, subsidising wage increases, putting in place (relatively minor) affirmative action provisions for Singaporeans in the job market and trying (yet again) to increase productivity,

---

[33] Lim, L. Y. C., & Lee, S. A. (2010). Globalizing State, Disappearing Nation: The Impact of Foreign Participation in the Singapore Economy. In T. Chong (Ed.), *Management of Success: Singapore Revisited* (pp. 139–158). Singapore: Institute of Southeast Asian Studies.

[34] Low, D., & Vadaketh, S. (2014). *Hard Choices: Challenging the Singapore Choices*. Singapore: NUS Press.

so far without success.[35] As noted on the Ministry of Manpower's website (MOM, n.d.)[36]:

> *Over the past decade, Singapore's economy grew by an average of 5% per annum. Singapore's productivity growth over the same period averaged about 1% per annum, a rate on par with that of other developed countries. The broad majority of Singaporeans also enjoyed real wage growth and a rise in living standards.*
>
> *Nonetheless, productivity gains have declined in recent years due to heavier reliance on labour inputs to generate economic growth, especially inputs of foreign manpower.*
>
> *Productivity is the only sustainable way to increase our value-add and grow our incomes and it must be the key driver of our economic growth. The Government will focus on helping businesses and workers improve their productivity and continue to provide support through many programmes and schemes.*

Significantly, the government has also announced a lowering of the target rate of GDP growth to 2% to 3% per year, similar to that in other developed countries, rather than the 3% to 5% (with 2% to 3% annual productivity growth) recommended by the Economic Strategies Committee in 2010 ("PM Lee redefines 'economy faring well'", 2015).[37] Clearly, it now accepts the limitations on growth imposed by domestic resource — and political — constraints, and maturity as a developed economy, which also undermine the continued viability of the "global city" model itself.[38] As I noted in a 2009 interview:

---

[35] Productivity dropped dramatically in 2014. See http://www.tradingeconomics.com/singapore/productivity.

[36] Ministry of Manpower (MOM). (n.d.). Skills, Training and Development. Ministry of Manpower. http://www.mom.gov.sg/employment-practices/skills-training-and-development.

[37] Lee, U.-W. (2014, January 17). PM Lee redefines 'economy faring well'. *The Business Times*. Retrieved from http://www.businesstimes.com.sg/government-economy/pm-lee-redefines-economy-faring-well.

[38] See *The Economist*. (2014, March 7). The world's most expensive city: Sing on a shoestring. Retrieved from http://www.economist.com/blogs/banyan/2014/03/world-s-most-expensive-city and Milman, O. (2015, January 5). The price of life in

Certainly, to generate growth, just by adding more input, you can get more output. But what is the opportunity cost? How much did we pay to attract such investment and what else might have been done with the money, tax revenue foregone and other local resources? Because we are a small economy, big, lumpy, capital-intensive investments that we do not control also increase our risk and our vulnerability to downturns, rather than protect us from them.

Ultimately, economic growth... should seek to increase the "income, welfare, stability and security of all Singaporeans". It should be "growth for people", not "people for growth".

In the long run, a lower rate of growth which delivers a higher ratio of benefits to Singaporeans may be more desirable than a higher rate of growth which is more unstable and inequitable. (Long, 2009a, p. 10)[39]

The global economic environment, so favourable in the first few decades after independence, is also very different today, presenting both challenges and opportunities for the future.

First, there will be a slowdown, if not a reversal, in the pace of globalisation in the next fifty years; world trade growth has fallen to, or below, world GDP growth, which it dramatically outpaced in previous decades (*The Economist,*

Singapore, city of rules: 'It's a Faustian deal'. *The Guardian.* Retrieved from http://www.theguardian.com/cities/2015/jan/05/the-price-of-life-in-singapore-city-of-rules-its-a-faustian-deal. While Singapore has been promoting urban density as a positive attribute of its "liveability" as a city, this does not mesh with studies that show a strong preference of rising middle classes in Asia, particularly China and India, major source countries for immigrants to Singapore, for more physical space, as reflected in growing suburban sprawl. See *The Economist.* (2014, December 6). A planet of suburbs: Places apart. All dense cities also have very low fertility rates, which I, and others have commented on in the Singapore context. Ever-increasing density, including through large-scale immigration, could thus compound Singapore's extreme demographic dilemma; see Lim, L. Y. C. (2014), How land and people fit together in Singapore's economy, in Low & Vadaketh, op. cit., pp. 31–47.

[39] Long, S. (2009a, March 11). Why it can't be more of the same. *The Straits Times.*

2014, December 13).[40] The reasons for what some have called "deglobalisation" include, on the supply side:

- Acceleration in shifts of comparative advantage, with automation in situ taking over from offshoring to more labour-intensive locations as manufacturing wages rise, whether in the US, where "reshoring" is picking up (*The Economist*, 2013, January 19)[41] or China, where electronics contract manufacturer Foxconn is planning to replace its one million workers with robots (*The Economist*, 2011, August 6)[42];

- Revolutionary technologies like 3-D printing enabling mass customisation and small-batch production at or close to where the final consumer resides (*The Economist*, 2013, September 7)[43];

- Continued shrinkage of the already fractional share of manufacturing in the value-chain of physical products like the Apple iPhone, most of whose value is embedded in services like design, marketing, software, retail and return to capital (of the roughly US$500 iPhone retail price in 2011, less than US$10 went to manufacturing in China) (Schuman, 2011)[44];

- Producing: where you sell to save on transport and inventory costs and turnaround time, and to reduce currency exposure and risk;

- Lower marginal benefits from further trade and investment liberalisation when most countries have already liberalised, with further liberalisation and standardisation more likely to occur on a regional than global level;

---

[40] *The Economist*. (2014, December 13). International Trade — A troubling trajectory. Retrieved from http://www.economist.com/news/finance-and-economics/21636089-fears-are-growing-trades-share-worlds-gdp-has-peaked-far.

[41] *The Economist*. (2013, January 19). Reshoring Manufacturing: Coming home. Retrieved from http://www.economist.com/news/special-report/21569570-growing-number-american-companies-are-moving-their-manufacturing-back-united.

[42] *The Economist*. (2011, August 6). Foxconn: Robots don't complain. Retrieved from http://www.economist.com/node/21525432.

[43] *The Economist*. (2013, September 7). 3-D printing scales up. Retrieved from http://www.economist.com/news/technology-quarterly/21584447-digital-manufacturing-there-lot-hype-around-3d-printing-it-fast.

[44] Schuman, M. (2011, May 16). Adding up the iPhone. *Time*. Retrieved from http://content.time.com/time/magazine/article/0,9171,2069042,00.html.

- Environmental and social policy pressures to reduce carbon footprints and thus streamline and shrink currently far-flung global supply chains;
- Narrowing of competitive advantage differences between geographies based on relative productivity levels, infrastructure and government incentives increasingly constrained by international agreements and protocols to "level the playing field", as economic development proceeds around the world.

On the demand side, we see:

- A slowdown in global macroeconomic growth as the rich world ages and stagnates and booming emerging markets become more mature;
- Manufacturing's shrinking and services' expanding share of value-added in global value-chains as world incomes rise, populations age and the heavily services-oriented "app economy" takes hold;
- Social innovations like the spread of the "sharing economy" (Lever, 2015)[45], the "on-demand economy" (*The Economist*, 2015, January 3)[46], conservation culture, buy-local norms and a values shift from material to experiential "goods" (like social media communications);
- A much lower rate of employment creation by large companies: for example, Facebook has annual revenues of US$12 billion and a market capitalisation exceeding US$200 billion but serves 1.5 billion customers with only 8,500 employees worldwide, most of whom are its home country.

All these add up to slower growth in output, a lower ratio of goods to services in output, a lower ratio of manufacturing to services value-added in goods, a greater localisation of goods and services production, and a much lower employment to output ratio, occurring at much lower levels of per capita income than in the present-day developed world. This is the post-industrial society on a global scale.

---

[45] Lever, R. (2015, February 3). 'Sharing economy' shapes markets as complaints rise. Agence France-Presse.
[46] *The Economist*. (2015, January 3). The Future of Work: There's an app for that. Retrieved from http://www.economist.com/news/briefing/21637355-freelance-workers-available-moments-notice-will-reshape-nature-companies-and.

For Singapore, these global trends indicate a need for transformation beyond the "global city" paradigm of the past fifty years. Today, there are also many more "global cities" competing for this role — Hong Kong, Shanghai, Sydney, Seoul — and more will emerge in the next fifty years. The gap in every dimension (physical infrastructure, income levels, social amenities, shopping, cultural activities) between the first-tier global cities of Shanghai and New York has dramatically narrowed while Shanghai's share of world GDP has increased as New York's has shrunk.[47] The same will eventually be true of the gap between Bangkok and Manila with that of Singapore.

Domestically, Singapore's comparative advantage long ago shifted decisively away from labour- to capital- and skills-intensity, despite decades of this market adjustment being slowed by compensating policy-created competitive advantages such as a liberal foreign-labour-and-talent policy. Such policy advantages will be increasingly difficult to sustain given heightened competition and spreading global norms like the reduced acceptability of tax-avoidance incentives for multinationals, a major feature of Singapore's attractiveness to foreign investors, many of whom would not locate here without them.[48]

However, is the real risk to Singapore that the age of the hub in MNC business models is coming under pressure and potentially to an end? A number of Beps proposals could make having a hub in somewhere like Singapore less palatable, if it means higher taxes on a global basis. For example, MNCs could end up paying more

---

[47] In 2000, China's share of world GDP was 3.6% while the U.S. share was 31%. By 2012, China's share had increased to 11% while the U.S. share had fallen to 22%. During this period, China's per capita income rose from 2.6% to 12.2% of the U.S's per capita income. See World Development Indicators at www.data.worldbank.org.

[48] I have heard this from many multinational subsidiaries in Singapore that I interviewed for my research. For the declining global acceptability of "tax arbitrage", see e.g., "EU to accuse Apple of taking illegal tax aid from Ireland", *The Guardian*, September 28, 2014; "More than 50 Countries Sign Tax Deal", *Wall Street Journal*, October 29, 2014; "UK Targets Tech Firms with 'Google Tax'", *Wall Street Journal*, December 3, 2014; "New Leak Shows Scope of Luxembourg Corporate-Tax Deals", *Wall Street Journal*, December 10, 2014; "EU to Widen Sweetheart Tax Deal Probe", *Wall Street Journal*, December 17, 2014.

in taxes when paying dividends from profitable subsidiaries with a hub in Singapore than if they had just paid to the headquarters directly. In that case, would this negate the operational benefits of having the hub in Singapore?

In a more extreme scenario, MNCs could choose to just invest into territories directly rather than through a hub location such as Singapore. This could be bad news for Singapore.[49] (Pickford, 2015)[50]

Changing US financial regulations such as those removing expatriate tax benefits, enforcing taxation of offshore bank accounts (under the Foreign Account Taxation Compliance Act, or FATCA) and imposing more restrictive credit rating standards on sovereign wealth funds like Temasek and GIC also impact Singapore's financial services sector ("Singapore isn't Greece, Singapore tells S&P in 29 pages", 2015).[51]

LOOKING TO SERVICES AND THE REGION

While Singapore's chosen development strategy of becoming a "global city" was the right one for its time and circumstances fifty years ago, the challenges of remaining internationally competitive in this role emerged rather quickly. It was only sixteen years after independence that Pang Eng Fong and I (1981)[52] wrote:

Ultimately, Singapore will have to face up to a fundamental strain in its domestic economy: the competition for labor between the services and the manufacturing sectors.

---

[49] Beps stands for the Base Erosion and Profit Shifting project that is being carried out by the Organisation for Economic Co-operation and Development (OECD). The current move towards corporate tax reform in the U.S., if effected, would also reduce the need for MNCs to shelter overseas income in offshore tax havens like Hong Kong, Singapore, Luxembourg, Ireland, Bermuda and the Cayman Islands.

[50] Pickford, B. (2015, January 27). Responsible taxation — the impact on Singapore's hub status. *The Business Times*. Retrieved from http://www.businesstimes.com.sg/opinion/responsible-taxation-the-impact-on-singapores-hub-status.

[51] *The Straits Times*. (2015, February 6). Singapore isn't Greece, Temasek tells S&P in 29 pages.

[52] Pang, E. F. & Lim, L. (1981, August 4) op. cit.

... Because of its labor-intensive base, and the rigidities imposed by fixed capital investments, restructuring in the manufacturing sector must be slow, and its success in the competitive international arena is by no means assured. The projected demands for high-skilled and experienced technical personnel are great and can't be met from the domestic labour pool. It's possible that they can't even be met internationally, given the shortages in skilled labour in most competing countries, including the advanced industrial nations.

... Singapore has a much stronger international competitive advantage in the export of services — banking, finance, commercial services, transportation, telecommunications — based on its long experience and large human and capital investment in these sectors. Another asset is its location in a rapidly growing regional economy of which it is the service hub. The service sector is intrinsically labor-intensive, and will become more skill-intensive as it upgrades into high-value services.

At the same time, even in export manufacturing industries, Singapore's competitiveness is shifting toward service-oriented activities such as regional warehousing, purchasing, servicing and research and development. Both commercial and industrial services have a demand for skilled professionals that can't be supplied adequately from domestic sources. And, as the Singapore population grows more affluent, it will consume more labor-intensive social and personal services than goods, further increasing the domestic demand for labor.

One solution to the long-range problem of labor shortage is to concentrate Singapore's limited domestic resources in the one area in which it has the greatest competitive advantage — the supply of services, including industrial-based services. This would mean the phasing out of production-oriented manufacturing, in which Singapore's potential advantage on a global basis is problematic.

Unskilled labor would be released for the nontraded services sector, and skilled labor would be available for professional jobs in the highly competitive traded services sector. Reliance on both unskilled and skilled foreign labor would be reduced, and Singapore's historic complementary role to countries in the region would be enhanced.

A few years later, the Report of the Economic Committee (1986) made similar recommendations:

[Singapore should] move beyond our being a production base, to being an international total business centre. We cannot depend only on companies coming to Singapore solely to make or assemble products designed elsewhere. We need to attract companies to Singapore to establish operational headquarters, which are responsible for subsidiaries throughout the region. In Singapore such headquarters should do product development work, manage their treasury activities, and provide administrative, technical and management services to their subsidiaries ...

Services account for an increasing share of our GDP, and our service exports have been growing as quickly as world trade in services. Scope for growth is still huge. We need to promote not just Singapore-based activities like tourism or banking, but also offshore-based activities, like construction firms building hotels in China, and salvage firms operating in the Middle East ... we have expertise in hotel management, air and sea port management, town and city planning. These skills should be systematically marketed ...

Our greatest potential for growth lies in this area: banking and finance, transport and communications, and international services. It has been growing rapidly.... The government must promote services actively, the same way it successfully promoted manufacturing.... Suitable incentives, including taxation of income from international services at a lower rate, will speed the shift toward a service economy. (As cited in Lee, 1989, p. 293)[53].

---

[53] Lee, S. A. (1989). Expansion of the Services Sector. In K. S. Sandhu and P. Wheatley (Eds.), *Management of Success: The Moulding of Modern Singapore* (pp. 280–299). Singapore: Institute of Southeast Asian Studies.

However, the committee did not recommend any reduction in the promotion of manufacturing:

> *As manufacturing is to be treated equally with services, there appears to be a continuity of the old pattern of concentrating on the overall growth rate as the target of economic policy and of emphasizing the visibility of manufacturing, despite the possibilities and the strength of the services sector.* (Lee, 1989, p. 297)[54]

Furthermore, the Economic Review Committee (2003) continued to emphasise manufacturing as one of the "twin engines" of GDP growth. Services continued to expand, growing from 60% of the GDP in 1985 and 1990 to 63% in 2005; its share of employment rose from 67% in 1990 to 77% in 2005 (Choy, 2010, p. 129)[55], enabled by the liberal foreign labour and talent policy as competition continued with the heavily-subsidised manufacturing sector for scarce resources. As the theory of *comparative* advantage tells us, a comparative advantage in one sector means a comparative *dis*advantage in another, and even large economies like the US and China cannot be equally competitive in every sector.

Choy (2010)[56] argues thus for a change in Singapore's economic model[57] away from manufacturing to services:

> *the service sector is less risky. Due to its very nature, service industries are less dependent on foreign capital and tend to be influenced to a smaller extent by business cycles. As Singapore establishes itself as a reputable exporter of final services such as financial wealth management, the media business, marketing and design services, tertiary education, and medical treatment — moving away from the current reliance on activities that are cyclically tied to manufacturing production such as intermediate trading, transportation, and banking services — the economy's vulnerability to external shocks will be reduced accordingly. The*

---

[54] Ibid.

[55] Choy, (2010) op. cit.

[56] Ibid.

[57] The definitive quantitative longitudinal study of the Singapore economy and its institutions is in Abeysinghe, T., & Choy, K. M. (2002).

construction of two world-class integrated resorts to attract high-spending visitors to Singapore can be construed as a step in this direction, though it must be acknowledged that international tourist traffic will remain sensitive to global economic conditions and geopolitical events.

More to the point, the development of a heterogeneous and diversified service sector offers the prospect that monetary policy will be a potent tool for mitigating economic fluctuations, as a result of the greater sensitivity of tradable services to exchange rate movements. Since exportable services have much higher domestic value-added and lower import content compared with manufactured goods, theory predicts and empirical evidence confirms that a currency depreciation stimulates the foreign demand for services much more than it does commodity exports.

For all this to come to pass, however, government bureaucrats need to intensify greatly their efforts to promote the service sector in general, and expand regional markets for tradable services in particular. Servicing the needs of the burgeoning middle classes in China and India could easily add a percentage point or two to Singapore's potential growth rate. One should also not neglect to mention the untapped potential of domestically-oriented service industries catering to a richer and ever-growing local population. Economic planners in Singapore must, therefore, shed their long-held bias in favour of manufacturing, stemming perhaps from the perception that service jobs are less glamorous and that the average level and growth rate of productivity in the service sector are lower compared with the goods industries. However, service industries have the virtue of being relatively labour-intensive, thus generating more employment and helping to keep both structural and cyclical unemployment at bay. The same cannot be said for high-technology manufacturing. For example, the biomedical sciences cluster currently accounts for only a small proportion of the workforce, its forward linkages with the health care industry notwithstanding. Moreover, if Singapore is going to be compared to the leading cities of the world such as New York and London, having a vibrant and progressive service sector will be essential for success....

... the manufacturing-based export growth engine which Singapore and other Asian economies have relied on so heavily for economic success has run out of steam and left them without domestic demand stabilizers. Therefore, it is time for the government to change Singapore's economic model to meet the new economic circumstances and challenges. (pp. 136–137)[58]

The next question one might ask is services for whom? The Strategic Economic Plan (1991) recommended the launch of what was called a "second wing" for the Singapore economy, encouraging local enterprises to venture out and invest in booming neighbouring countries, with the assistance of government fiscal incentives, tax concessions, equity financing and infrastructure provision to support overseas ventures.

By 1997, S$75.8 billion in cumulative outward direct investments had been committed by local firms, though the lion's share was, not surprisingly, attributed to government-linked companies (GLCs).

Sadly, though, the Asian financial crisis erupted in July 1997 with the devaluation of the Thai baht and brought to a dramatic end the golden era of strong regional and domestic economic growth that had lasted for nearly a decade. (Choy, 2010, p. 126)[59]

Despite this slowdown, both large and small Singapore companies have continued to invest abroad, with Asia their top source of overseas revenue, and ASEAN particularly important for SMEs.[60] Recently, Dr Teh Kok Peng

---

[58] Choy, (2010), op. cit.
[59] Ibid.
[60] See "Asia remains biggest source of overseas revenue for Singapore companies", *The Straits Times*, January 29, 2015, citing the Singapore International 100 ranking by the DP Group.

(2014)[61] has called for "creating a second Singapore outside Singapore" (as cited in Teh, 2014):[62]

> *while the particular globalization strategy that Singapore embarked on soon after independence was the right one ... we may have overstayed in applying this strategy as the dominant one. As a result, our shortage of land, labour and other capabilities is becoming more obvious and severe. I believe it is time to have a second strategic pillar, which I would describe in short as "creating a second Singapore outside Singapore." ... the economic space of Singapore and Singapore companies should be much bigger than the geographical space of Singapore....*

> *Singapore's land and labour constraints are immutable. Since independence in 1965, our planners have done a remarkable job in land reclamation and urban planning such that we have been able to increase our population and the intensity of our land use without the residents feeling unduly overcrowded or congested until recent years.... Nevertheless, in the long term, there is clearly a limit as to how much more we can do in land use intensification, given how much we have already done.*

> *With regard to labour, Singapore had actually run up against domestic labour constrains early on, and had begun importing foreign workers, mainly Malaysians, by the early 1970s.... Since then, our dependence rate of foreign workers as a proportion to our total work force has risen sharply, to possibly the highest in the world, with the exception of the Gulf States.... It is this surge in our resident population ... that has given rise to ... discontent.*

> *... It may well be that Singapore can support a population of 6.9 million without being congested or over-crowded, with clever planning and after the current massive construction of MRTs, highways, hospitals, schools, HDBs etc. all reach completion. But*

---

[61] Teh, op. cit.

[62] Dr Teh, an economist, was President of the Government of Singapore Investment Corporation (GIC) Special Investments division from 1999–2011, and is currently a non-executive director of several large Singapore companies.

it may also be the case that one man's buzz is another man's claustrophobia.

The question also arises as to the marginal benefit of such further large capital investments in a limited space and ... with the limited supply of labour. In economic theory, when one factor of production — land — is largely fixed, and another factor — labour — can only grow slowly, adding more and more capital leads to diminishing returns. About twenty years ago, Paul Krugman argued that Singapore's growth ... was largely driven by inputs of labour and capital rather than productivity. If this is true, are we in the process of doing more of the same, even if the declared intent is to develop a more innovation-based, productivity-driven economy? (pp. 100–101)

Dr Teh goes on to note that more mature developed economies are all large importers *and* exporters of foreign direct investment, which yields higher returns than the portfolio investments in which Singapore currently concentrates its massive foreign reserves (resulting from high savings and large cumulative budget and current account surpluses, managed mainly by MAS and GIC). Given this large stock of accumulated capital and other capabilities, and a per capita income that is one of the world's highest, a "second Singapore" is clearly feasible as well as desirable. Income from foreign investments would also help counter the long-term balance-of-payments outflow of investment income from the huge stock of inward foreign direct investment in Singapore itself. In Dr Teh's opinion, "it seems to me that we are at a stage of development where the greater risk by far is not venturing out".[63]

Such outward direct investment has the following benefits: easing the pressure on Singapore's own land and labour market, as foreign labour is employed in their home countries instead; enabling SMEs to achieve scale more easily and deploy their developed technologies and capabilities more profitably in lower-cost locations; avoiding potential exclusion from promising markets, and acquiring new knowledge and capabilities abroad that could be transferred to enhance parent firms' competitive advantages; and higher returns

---

[63] Comment made at IPS Singapore Perspectives 2015.

on investments enabling the payment of higher taxes to help fund the domestic transfer payments put into place to serve growing social needs.

Fortunately, in addition to the physical, financial and human capital built up over the past fifty years, Singapore benefits from an excellent geographical location in the centre of South-east Asia. This is the next large emerging regional market to which global multinationals are already turning their investment attention, as are Singapore and national companies in our neighbouring countries.[64] The tapering off (*note:* not total disappearance) of the 20th-century development model of manufacturing for export through multinational networks to rapidly-ageing, slowly-growing, distant rich markets will be replaced by domestic consumption-led growth in faster-growing nearby middle-income markets like China (as it "rebalances" its economy away from the current investment-driven export-led manufacturing model towards increased domestic consumption of services)[65] and the more youthful India and Indonesia. Singapore's well-developed industrial services referred to above can also integrate with developing manufacturing capabilities in neighbouring countries, for both regional and global markets

Singapore can build on our natural differentiating advantages versus other "global cities" by playing a role in regional value-chains catering to the hundreds of millions who are already entering the middle class all around us. Based on comparative (capital, skills) and competitive advantage (infrastructure, first-comer advantage, location, culture), our edge is likely to be in value-added services — finance, education, health-and-wellness, recreation — that we already provide to the world's and region's wealthy, and which market research studies already show strong demand growth for in these

---

[64] See, for example, "Indonesia sees surge in foreign investment", *Wall Street Journal*, January 20, 2012; "Foxconn moves into Indonesia, worrying labor groups", *Christian Science Monitor*, September 5, 2012; "Indonesia to Big Chains: Share the wealth", *Wall Street Journal*, May 12, 2013; "Facebook.ers in Indonesia Rise to 69 million", *Wall Street Journal*, June 27, 2014; "Japan Inc. goes deeper into Southeast Asia" (*Wall Street Journal*, September 28, 2014; "Japanese Investment in Southeast Asia: Outward bound", *Economist*, November 1, 2014.

[65] This is the same economic model that Singapore should also rebalance away from. See Lim, L. Y. C. (2010). Rebalancing in East Asia. In S. Claessens, S. Evenett and B. Hoekman (Eds.), *Rebalancing the Global Economy: A Primer for Policymaking* (pp. 32–35). London: Centre for Economic Policy-Making.

markets.[66] What we need to do is cater more explicitly to the much larger numbers just slightly further down the regional income distribution, who are likely to consume similar services and at similar price-points to the bottom 80% of our local citizens by income level, who can provide and benefit from such services themselves as skill capabilities and scale economies develop.

Put simply, we will move from manufacturing physical goods for customers richer than we are to providing services to customers poorer than we are. The good news is that services for our regional neighbourhood are more location-specific and scalable, and less capital- and energy-intensive, than manufacturing for distant markets, less reliant on rare specific technical skills unlikely to be found in adequate scale among our small population and more open to small entrepreneurs with different levels of formal education, providing a channel for employment creation, upward mobility and reduced inequality (through SME ownership and the capital returns from operating in regional markets). As I have written elsewhere:

> In both high-tech manufacturing and financial services, Singapore lacks not just market scale and supply-chain depth and diversity, but also a sizeable globally-competitive labour and talent pool. So far it has succeeded by importing the narrowly specific skill sets that these sectors require — like electronics engineers from China and financial and IT experts from India — but this has already bumped up against … constraints. In the next 50 years it will also become more difficult to attract top talent from other Asian countries as their economies develop, giving their talented citizens better career opportunities and lifestyles at home.
>
> Fortunately, Singapore's scale also confers certain advantages, in that it only needs to excel (on the supply side) in relatively few, smaller but higher-value, product niches in order to compete globally and provide sufficient employment opportunities for its

---

[66] Some examples include McKinsey (March 2012), "Meet the Chinese Consumer of 2020"; Accenture (February 2013), "Meet the New Chinese Consumer"; Boston Consulting Group (March 2013), "Indonesia's Rising Middle Class and Affluent Consumers".

resident population, with the help (on the demand side) of expanded domestic consumption by the local population, and demand from increasingly affluent regional neighbours. Looking forward 50 years, two major intrinsic assets that the country possesses are its geographical location in the centre of what will be the world's largest fast-growing middle-income regional market (the currently 600-plus million in Southeast Asia, together with the 1.5 billion-plus in South Asia), and its own population's cultural affinity with the populations in that market, which will be particularly important in various professional, personal and social services.

In financial services, for example, the principle of portfolio diversification alone will dictate that some segment of the burgeoning mass middle classes of Southeast Asia will place some portion of their savings in or with Singapore-based financial institutions and finance professionals, just as high-net-worth individuals from the region and the world already do. In tourism, there is already a large and vibrant regional market, which will only grow as more families are able to afford short holidays in neighbouring countries. Health and educational services are already well-developed and have further room to grow, especially for average-income customers. (Lim, 2015, p. 101)[67]

Note that Indonesia is already the largest source of international visitors to Singapore, followed (at some distance) by China, while elder services (that Singapore's rapidly-expanding ranks of elderly could also benefit from at home) are already beginning to take off in China ("China's aging boomers are lucrative market", 2015).[68] From a trade policy perspective, for all its likely disappointments, the ASEAN Economic Community, which is due to be

---

[67] Lim, L. Y. C. (2015). Singapore in the International Economy. In E. Quah (Ed.), *Singapore 2065: Leading Insights on the Economy and Environment from 50 Singapore Icons and Beyond.* Singapore: World Scientific (pp. 98–102).
[68] Burkitt, L. (2015, January 20). China's aging boomers are lucrative market. *Wall Street Journal.*

launched by the end of 2015 (ASEAN Secretariat, 2014)[69], will enhance the prospects for regional services integration, given its vision of a "single market" for services, regulatory standardisation, infrastructural connectivity (e.g. in telecommunications, to facilitate e-commerce) and promotion of SMEs and SME collaboration.

What of the role of state industrial and social policy, which I argued above was critical to the success of the post-independence "global city" economic model? This transition from being one of many global cities to becoming a one-of-a-kind regional city requires shifts in Singaporean mindsets, educational choices, labour market behaviours and government policies that directly or indirectly influence and incentivise them.

> *Focusing on employment and income creation for the average native Singaporean as opposed to income maximisation for footloose foreign corporations ... requires a shift in economic policy and individual thinking from, among others, the global to regional, manufacturing to services, capital to labour and skills, high-end to middle, foreign to local, state to market, large to small, profits to wages, corporate to entrepreneurial, and so on.*
> (Lim, 2015, p. 101)

Given the strong underlying market advantages, I do not see a role for state industrial policy to micro-manage this shift. Rather, I would propose a downsizing, if not dismantling, of the whole bureaucratic infrastructure that has for decades strived — with some, if incomplete and declining, success — to "manage" Singapore's international competitiveness as a "global city", particularly in manufacturing. Not only is such state management of competitiveness no longer effective or even possible in the changed global environment that is already with us today, but it also distorts resource allocation at home and abroad, discouraging entrepreneurial investments. A reduction in the role of state intervention in the forces of dynamic comparative and competitive advantage would, among other things, release scarce resources of capital and local talent to find their way into the most market-advantageous economic activities which I, and others, have argued are likely to be in services

---

[69] ASEAN Secretariat. (May 2014). *Thinking Globally, Prospering Regionally— ASEAN Economic Community 2015*. Jakarta: ASEAN.

for the domestic and regional market, a process which is already taking place. As noted in my 2009 interview:

> The way forward for Singapore... is to allow the market to 'diversify on its own', with resource allocation done by market forces and entrepreneurs, instead of the state and bureaucrats.
>
> Do we devote our carefully husbanded national savings, accumulated over generations, to letting the state make big bets on a few major, capital-intensive, risky and expensive projects?
>
> Or do we privatize the economy, releasing capital and talent to local entrepreneurs to create value in smaller but nimbler enterprises? At least, if they fail, it will take only small parts, rather than big chunks, of the economy down with them.
>
> It's much better to send out 100 motorboats, rather than one huge aircraft carrier, into the unknown. I would bet on at least some of the motorboats making it, instead of the aircraft carrier, a sitting duck, which could get blown up. (Long, 2009b, p. 10)[70]

I have been visiting Myanmar for thirty years. About eight years ago, I interviewed some Singaporean businesses there and found to my surprise and delight that there were already about 350 of them, mostly SMEs in services like trading, schools, hair salons, small hotels, shops and restaurants. This was well before Myanmar started opening out to foreign investment in 2011, after which Singapore GLCs, banks and government agencies like International Enterprise Singapore (IE) and SingBridge, as well as MNCs from many countries, moved in in a big way. Our SMEs had ventured into a very difficult business environment ahead of most of the "big boys", and they were doing well.

Since the 1991 "second wing" initiative, many of our GLCs have also ventured into the region. Mr Chow Yew Yuen, CEO of Keppel Offshore and Marine, shared his company's experience:

---

[70] Long, S. (2009b, March 11). New growth model beyond Jack-of-all-hubs needed. *The Straits Times*.

As offshore and marine, we operate in 15 countries and we have 20 yards worldwide. Most of our operations we manage with a few Singaporeans. We find that Singaporeans are actually, because of our background, able to operate in those countries quite well if you compare with people of maybe more homogeneous societies like the Japanese or the Koreans.… In our case, we are moving a lot of our less skill intensive types of operation overseas. For example, we have moved to the Philippines, Indonesia and some of the other regional places. But to protect the mothership, we are consciously making decisions on where we keep our R&D development, our project management development and our supply chain management (in Singapore).[71]

Individual Singaporean entrepreneurs have also ventured into our South-east Asian neighbours.

One example is Kwok Kian Tow, a Singaporean economist-by-training whose company runs granite quarries and processing facilities in Singapore, Malaysia and China, branching out into construction materials in Vietnam and Myanmar, and into property development in Malaysia and China. His company also manufactures die-cast aluminium parts in Malaysia. To quote Kwok:

The British East India Company sent ordinary Englishmen to the 'Far East' and many became leading businessmen thousands of miles away from home. Each of us who went away from Singapore shores to do business in Southeast Asian countries and beyond had an EIC "eureka moment" — that these lands held opportunities equal to or better than home. As for the drive and the flow to do business in unfamiliar settings, most of us had no EIC to give us a start, a leg up. Each had his own story.[72]

Some younger Singaporeans are also doing the same thing, and for the same reason, namely, they see the Singapore market as "saturated".

---

[71] Comment made at the post-panel discussion at IPS Singapore Perspectives 2015 on 26 January 2015.

[72] Kwok Kian Tow, personal communication with author in February 2015.

And Sharifah Yuhaniz, a Singaporean MBA entrepreneur in Malaysia, says:

In my business, the opportunities are in South East Asia. With lower oil prices, many downstream projects like in situ small-scale power generation projects are becoming viable and are taking off. Especially in an archipelago of small land masses like South East Asia, producing power near demand makes a lot more sense than dealing with expensive transmission.[73]

Social policy could also have a role to play in enabling or encouraging more Singaporeans to become entrepreneurs, develop service enterprises and venture into Southeast Asia. For example, if Singaporeans did not have to devote so much of their savings to CPF and housing, they would have more disposable income and time to spend on consuming domestic services,[74] creating jobs at home and accumulating start-up capital and developing capabilities that could be invested both at home and abroad. They might even be able to marry at a younger age, have more children and be able to support themselves in their post-retirement years ("Top concerns for Singaporeans", 2015)[75]. A universal social safety net for poverty and pension relief might reduce the risk aversion that discourages entrepreneurial activity. And educational options could be increased at all age levels to provide experiences (e.g. active learning projects in neighbouring countries) and skills (e.g. studying South-east Asian languages, non-university accounting, finance and marketing courses) that would

---

[73] Sharifah Yuhaniz, personal communication with author on 23 February 2015.

[74] Tilak Abeysinghe and Choy Keen Meng, "The aggregate consumption puzzle in Singapore", *Journal of Asian Economics* 15 (2004), pp. 563–578; Tilak Abeysinghe and Jiaying Gu, "Lifetime income and housing affordability in Singapore", *Urban Studies* 48 (2011), pp. 1875–1901; Linda Lim and James Cheng, "Why Singapore is not Iceland", *The Business Times*, Singapore, January 24, 2014; "'Meaningful correction still unachieved': Tharman", *The Business Times*, October 29, 2014; "Not kicking the habit", *Economist*, February 7, 2015, all refer to the high level of household debt in Singapore. In contrast, in the U.S., entrepreneurs often resort to home mortgages for start-up capital.

[75] Channel NewsAsia. (2015, February 16). Top concerns for Singaporeans: Retirement adequacy, healthcare and cost of living. *Channel News Asia*, Retrieved from http://www.channelnewsasia.com/news/singapore/top-concerns-for/1663084.html.

encourage and enable entrepreneurship.[76] Given vested (and competing) interests, including entrenched bureaucratic interests, and the multiple other needs that social policy must fulfil, bold policy changes are unlikely here.

CONCLUSION

The "global city" model served Singapore's economic development well in the early decades of independence when it comported well with the country's mostly market-based comparative and competitive advantages. As these changed, strategic government industrial and social policy interventions managed to preserve international competitiveness, mostly by importing foreign capital, talent, labour and technology to serve global markets. However, this was at the cost of ever-increasing subsidies for foreign investors ("corporate welfare"), distortions and rigidities in the allocation of resources, disappointing productivity growth, increased volatility, inequality and negative externalities, and the "crowding out" of local entrepreneurs and non-favoured sectors, calling into question the model's continued economic, social and political sustainability.

Looking forward to the next fifty years, dramatic and rapid changes in the global economy further undermine the viability of the "global city" model. However, a fortunate geography, and valuable national assets accumulated over the past half-century, provides Singapore with a new opportunity to prosper as a regional city serving the growing service consumption needs of the increasingly wealthy middle classes of South-east and South Asia, and connecting them with the wider world as necessary. This transition requires an entrepreneurial spirit that will enable us to create our own jobs rather than slot ourselves into the declining number of jobs that will emanate from large foreign companies. In addition, a mindset shift in geographical orientation is required:

> For the last 40 years, Singapore has viewed itself as 'an outpost of Western empire, catering to those scared of the jungle and needing an intermediary'...

---

[76] For a more extended discussion of what Singapore and Singaporeans can do to prepare for the employment challenges of the present and future, see Lim, L. Y. C. (2014), What's wrong with Singaporeans? In Low & Vadaketh, op. cit. pp. 79–96.

... Instead of trying to be a 'secondary global node', Singapore should focus on being a 'primary regional one' and leverage its 'unique location-specific advantages'. (Long, 2009a, p. 10)[77]

From the 1910s to the 1930s, my great-grandfather Kung Tian Siong, the first of now six generations of my family to study in Anglo-Chinese School (and, beginning with my great-grandmother, Methodist Girls' School), frequently travelled to and readily conducted business in cities as diverse as Batavia (now Jakarta), Surabaya, Pontianak and Shanghai on the one hand, and Los Angeles, Chicago, New York, London and Frankfurt on the other, while his younger brother Kung Tian Cheng lived and worked for some years in Bangalore and Mysore as well as Penang, Shanghai and Beijing. Their widowed mother was an illiterate seamstress who spoke only dialect, yet both men became fluent and literate in English, Malay, Mandarin and several Chinese dialects, and were clearly comfortable in many different cultural milieus.[78] There have always been Singaporeans like them, and there should be many more in our next fifty years, as we increase the regional, while retaining the global, content and context of our city, and of our nation's economy. Conserving our multicultural national identity will then go hand in hand with economic progress and social well-being.

For more, please refer to:

Lim, L. Y. C. (May 2009). Singapore's Economic Growth Model: Too Much or Too Little?" *Ethos, 6,* 32–38.

Pang, E. F., & Lim, L. (1989). High Tech and Labour in the Asian NICs. *Labour and* Society, *14,* 43–57.

---

[77] Long, (2009a) op. cit.
[78] For more details on their lives and careers, see Lim, L. Y. C. (2014). *Four Chinese Families in British Colonial Malaya: Confucius, Christianity and Revolution* (3rd Ed.). Retrieved from www.blurb.com. Also available at the National, NUS and ISEAS libraries in Singapore.

3

Debate

5

Pragmatism Should Be Retained As Singapore's Governing Philosophy

KISHORE MAHBUBANI, TONG YEE,
VIKRAM KHANNA AND EUGENE K B TAN

The motion for the Singapore Perspectives 2015 debate was "This conference resolves that pragmatism remains important and should be retained as our governing philosophy". During the course of the debate, members of the audience were invited to use their polling devices to vote for either the Proposition or the Opposition. The debate was chaired by Ms Debra Soon, Head of News Segment at MediaCorp.

Chairperson: Good afternoon, ladies and gentlemen. Welcome to the first "post-lunch slump" session of Singapore Perspectives 2015. I will do my best to keep the session moving along so you don't fall asleep but it will mainly be up to the erudite speakers to scintillate you as they debate a rather complex and convoluted motion. I have to say though, only a mind similarly complex and convoluted as Mr Janadas Devan's could have come up with this. The motion reads: "This conference resolves that pragmatism remains important and should be retained as our governing philosophy". Now since Mr Devan has arm-twisted me into this, I thought I could crack a joke at his expense. Actually maybe two, so if I'm not here next year, you all will know the reason why.

Now, to me, the motion assumes several things. First, that pragmatism is currently in place, is a governing philosophy and is ours, in other words, shared. Is pragmatism really a philosophy? Is this what has driven us as a collective and as a people? Or does this refer to the government, or the ruling party or both? Is it whatever works? Do policy efficiencies and outcomes justify pragmatic means? Has it always been our governing philosophy or has this evolved over the years? These are some thoughts to ponder. I'm sure our speakers will enlighten us. Here is a little on the format. We will have opening remarks, five minutes for each team, followed by a challenge and rebuttal round. The questions will be one-minute long and responses two minutes each. We will have four rounds.

It is my pleasure to introduce the teams to you. For the Proposition, we have Mr Tong Yee, Director of The Thought Collective, and Professor Kishore Mahbubani, Dean of Lee Kuan Yew School of Public Policy. For the Opposition, we have Mr Vikram Khanna, Associate Editor of *Business Times*, and Associate Professor Eugene Tan, School of Law, Singapore Management University. You have seen all of them on television and they are experts. The first thing that I have to do is to ask all of you to vote on the poll question — which is a bit sharper than the motion — "Pragmatism should be retained as Singapore's governing philosophy". Those of you who agree, in other words with the Proposition, vote "1" and send it in. Those of you who disagree, press "2" and send it in.

1ST VOTING RESULT:
PROPOSITION — 72.9%, OPPOSITION — 27.1%

Chairperson: Nearly 73 per cent feel that pragmatism has to be retained as our governing philosophy. Without further ado, I will now invite the first speaker of the Proposition, Tong Yee, to make his opening remarks. Tong Yee, your time starts now.

Tong Yee: Good afternoon. Honestly, the sheer fact that I'm standing here at the IPS Singapore Perspectives Conference debating with the brightest minds in Singapore is perhaps one of the least pragmatic things I've agreed to do in the past few years. Being a two-time repeat student, and having only earned a pass degree at NUS, this being in Theatre Studies mind you, I really do not know what insane and logical point I'm trying to prove by potentially making a fool of myself on national TV. So in preparation for this, I had time to seriously reflect and consider and I came to the conclusion that if I'm going to make the best of this learning opportunity, if I'm going to use this platform to make some profoundly poignant points that will somehow make Singapore proud, then I might as well win while I'm doing it, which is why I'm on Kishore's side and not the other side.

But that really is a point in itself. I've been a social entrepreneur for over a decade now, and when IPS first invited me to be a debater in this conference, I was politely given a choice of which side I would prefer to argue on. I chose to argue for pragmatism. Five to six years ago, I would even have surprised myself. One would think that social entrepreneurs are bold, innovative radicals, full of ideals and having a genuine desire to serve the community and do so in a very sustainable way. It is a bold and compelling dream and immensely fashionable among young people today. But at least in part, these ideals have held true for me, but maybe not so much in recent years.

The path of social entrepreneurship, if anything, has been a real education on the profound value of pragmatism. For me at least, there is a grounding principle on which I choose to live. I learnt very quickly in my very own pursuit of ideals that I really shouldn't keep falling from my own heights. Saving the world, wanting equality for all, making Singapore a place where people could all have equal opportunity, these were some things that I felt I needed to contribute to, partly due to my own suffering as I grew up as a young person in Singapore. But being able to deliver on that particular promise, on that particular social promise, to retain the integrity of being able to serve others is something that I quickly learnt was dependent upon sound financial principles, a strong grasp of reality, the accurate reading of current market conditions and, yes, taking into account the myriad personalities and working partners and collaborators that we have to somehow begin to work with. And if I genuinely wanted to pursue a career, to live my ideals, then I must first ground that in the practical reality. It's not the most popular thing to say, but one I believe we all have to hear and maybe have the courage to follow.

Make no mistake, we need idealism, we need inspiration and we need values. But pragmatism and us believing and wanting to achieve a world that is better than the one we currently have are not mutually exclusive. Rather it is pragmatism that remains a foundation for idealism. In the same way that it was our parents and pioneer generation that focused on pragmatic jobs that gave us, perhaps, the ability to follow our ideals today. It is very much similar to a generation of shipyard workers that followed, that allowed for today's cupcake makers. I do not find pragmatism to be an option that invites cynicism. In fact, pragmatism demands exceptional leadership and moral courage.

Pragmatism is not an expedient reading of any one given context and simply adapting ourselves to suit the demands of the times. Pragmatism is the reading of all contexts. It includes the moral one, financial one, political one, the cultural one and, yes, the sustainable one. And I have come to a conclusion that it's really the way of seeing things which perhaps would guarantee us the best success in the long game. Can the government stand against inequalities when the very nature of the world is unequal? I know that these are key narratives for campaigns and even elections. But for governance, I'm not so sure. I've found that when governments start wearing the underpants on the outside of the red and blue leotard and start flying around fighting for causes, they tend to look very ridiculous, at least eventually. No matter how hard I want to believe that we have shaken off the fact that we remain one of the smallest nation states in the world.

Has our success in supplying water for ourselves deceived us into thinking that we have somehow resolved the food problem or our complete dependence on others for food? Have our stellar education and the fact that we can hold debates in fancy hotels convinced us that our thoughts and perspectives are some things that will even be heard in a politically mired landscape? When push comes to shove, can Singapore really afford to push back and somehow still keep these wings on which we fly? Pragmatism is hardly popular, rarely inspiring and oftentimes sobering. But what it guarantees is that pragmatic leaders are grounded in realities and not ideologies. Thank you.

Chairperson: Thank you, Tong Yee. Can I now invite the first speaker for the Opposition, Vikram, to speak?

Vikram Khanna: Good afternoon, ladies and gentlemen, I have to say that were it not for Janadas' persuasive powers, I would not be here. I am participating in this debate with some trepidation. I mean, to argue against pragmatism in the context of Singapore is like arguing against motherhood, as you can see from the voting results. I have just five minutes so I can only sketch some broad themes, which I hope we can flesh out a little later. One doesn't oppose pragmatism. It is good. I think the first part of the motion is taken. Pragmatism is useful by definition. But the motion says it should be retained as our governing philosophy, not that it should be an important element in our governing philosophy, nor that our governing philosophy should be tempered with pragmatism but pragmatism should be it. That is it and nothing else. Now that kind of sticks in my throat a little bit.

I don't know if you saw the interview that the Prime Minister gave to the media a few days ago when he was asked about pragmatism and he said pragmatism is good, whatever works is good. But there are certain things that are what he calls "unshakeable". The rule of law, meritocracy, interethnic harmony, these are there forever, not out of pragmatism but because they are good intrinsically in and of themselves. And I think that there are certain things in life that are good intrinsically in and of themselves.

The other word in the motion that I have a problem with is that we should retain pragmatism. As if we have always been pragmatic. I know a lot of things have been sold as pragmatism, packaged as pragmatism, framed as being pragmatic. But I think we need to raise a few questions as to whether they really have been. I can say this in the context of, just to give a few examples which I hope we can flesh out later, our approach to welfare, housing, immigration and education, and our approach to information. These are some of the areas where I think we have sometimes been short of being pragmatic.

The other issue I have with the motion is pragmatism for whom? What is pragmatic for me might not be pragmatic for you. You can say pragmatic for society yes, but I think as society becomes more diverse and more complex, it becomes a much more difficult proposition to deliver on. There are also issues relating to our economic policy of the past; I think we have taken some very bold, visionary, radical steps. Our pro-multinational industrialisation programme of the 1960s went against the ruling paradigm of the time. We took big, bold bets in areas such as semiconductors and biotech. Some of these were quite radical decisions. In retrospect, they may appear to be pragmatic, but at the time when the decisions were made, they certainly were not. Some of them were leaps in the dark.

When we talk about the economy, we also need to look at the future, we need to look at innovation, we need to look at creativity, and these require things beyond just pragmatism. I hope we will be able to make a case for that.

But at the end of the day, I think I hope we can make the case that yes, pragmatism is important, but it also needs to be accompanied by other things, by idealism, inspiration, principle, conviction and a moral compass. Pragmatism alone is not enough.

I think I would recast the motion to say we need a pragmatic approach to our governing philosophy. That is completely different from saying pragmatism should be our governing philosophy. What it means is yes, we have elements of pragmatism but we also have elements of principle, we also have elements of morality and elements of conviction, and we also have elements of compassion and justice. If we say pragmatism alone should be our governing philosophy, I think we are elevating pragmatism itself to the level of an ideology — and that is not very pragmatic!

Chairperson: Thank you, Vikram. We're going to start what we call the response and challenge round, or the challenge round. I'd like to invite the first person from the proposing team to issue the challenge. Kishore, you have one minute.

Kishore Mahbubani: Thank you, Vikram. I am glad you said that pragmatism is like motherhood. So please do not vote against your mother in the final round. You said that we should have balanced pragmatism with morality and with idealism, implying that they sort of exclude each other. But you know, Mr S Rajaratnam said many years ago — and I quote — "Unsentimental pragmatism has made life more human, more dignified, and more hopeful for Singaporeans". So what could be more moral and more idealistic than what Mr Rajaratnam has spelt out?

Chairperson: Eugene, I need you to respond to that question from Kishore.

Eugene Tan: I think it's important to recognise that when we talk about pragmatism here, we are concerned about pragmatism being elevated to a point where we do not consider other imperatives. So putting it another way, it is not just about getting to the summit of the mountain but fundamentally about *how* we get to the summit. Are we going to leave people behind in that pursuit? We should not underestimate the importance of morality, principles and values. The shared purpose will always be there, but how do we discipline that shared purpose? We take the view that pragmatism alone is not enough; if anything; unbridled pragmatism will get us into a lot of trouble.

This is where we are coming from, and we need to recognise the imperative for pragmatism to be balanced. We are not saying do away with pragmatism. We are saying that we need to be even-handed. We need to be pragmatic but we also certainly need to look at concerns, particularly at this stage of our development where our material needs are more or less satisfied. We need to go beyond those material needs and engage the aspirations. How do we build a nation when everyone is driven by pragmatic considerations? How do we create a national soul? How do we get people to feel that this is a place where we will stay regardless of whether things are good or bad? We take the view that pragmatism alone will do us in. Pragmatism will get us through the day but we need more than pragmatism to get us through the night. As a society, we need to go beyond material concerns to incorporating post-material aspirations as well.

Chairperson: Thank you. Now you have a minute to issue a challenge to the proposing team.

Eugene Tan: The Proposition has presented pragmatism as something workable. Vikram and I do not disagree with that. But isn't pragmatism ultimately ideological? That, in the end, pragmatism will actually kill any discussion as it prevents us from looking at alternatives. Well, because what is pragmatic is the path we take. It tells us to focus solely on what works. But it does not tell us how it works, how we are going to get there. So the question for the Proposition is: How are we going to build a nation? If we have people who treat this place like a hotel, people will say, "Well, it does not make sense for me to stay here any longer. I might as well get up and go". Then the past 50 years would have been a waste. Thank you.

Chairperson: Thank you. Tong Yee, you are going to respond. You have two minutes starting from now.

Tong Yee: I think one of the things that amazes me most is that and this goes with my experience — I have just come from one of our ITEs [Institutes of Technical Education], that is ITE Central, and I remember while growing up in Singapore, I wondered why Singapore did not have a sense of equality or justice and why we stereotyped one group over another. But stepping into that ITE campus earlier, I met youths speaking to me with confidence and dignity. I am proud of the fact that we have, our country has, built such a facility. And I would say that the ITE itself is idealism. It is idealism to create equal education for all. But I do remember that it took us some time to get there. So when we are pragmatic, we begin to build things. I really think that it is a question of time and that in time itself you will begin to see that with a foundation of pragmatism, you eventually will be able to fulfil, I guess, all the idealisms that we do stand for as a nation.

Chairperson: You have another forty-seven seconds if you want to continue before you challenge.

Tong Yee: I don't have anything else to say.

Chairperson: If not, carry on issuing the challenge to the opposing team now.

Kishore Mahbubani: Thank you. The most surprising thing you said was that pragmatism, at the end of the day, is an ideology. As far as I know, that is a contradiction. An ideological approach is the opposite of a pragmatic one, if you follow what ideology says and what pragmatism says. It was John Kenneth Galbraith who said, "I react pragmatically. Where the market works, I'm for that; where the government is necessary, I'm for that. I'm deeply suspicious of somebody who says I'm in favour of privatisation or in favour of government". That is ideology. How can you confuse ideology with pragmatism?

Chairperson: Thank you, Kishore.

Vikram Khanna: I will speak on behalf of Eugene. I think, just to clarify, that an ideology is when somebody says pragmatism alone should be a governing principle, pragmatism and nothing else. That has the effect of elevating pragmatism to the level of an ideology. And I think that's a fair statement to make.

Chairperson: Eugene, would you like to respond as well? You have more time.

Eugene Tan: Since Professor Kishore Mahbubani quoted an economist, let me quote an economist in return. Douglass North said that strong moral and ethical codes of a society are the cement of social stability, which makes an economic system viable. In the end, it is important to look beyond pragmatism that is required in a given situation. What is it that we hope to get out of a certain policy? You said that pragmatism is not an ideology. But I would submit that it is an ideology simply because it tells you how to go about doing things, working on a basis of what works.

Chairperson: You now have some time to issue a challenge to the proposition team.

Vikram Khanna: Kishore, I will be a little kinder to you than you were to us. As you are a foreign policy expert, I will ask you a question on foreign policy. Singapore supported the Iraq war, which was a violation of international law and also a violation of the UN Charter. Was that pragmatic? And was that right?

Kishore Mahbubani: I must say that is an excellent question. The simple answer is that it was a good, pragmatic decision on the part of Singapore to support the Iraq war. Because if you look at the foreign policy alternatives that Singapore had at that time — what choices it had and what it had to do — it was clear that, on balance, it was better for Singapore to support the Iraq war. Many of you probably do not know about the remarkable amount of benefits that Singapore has gained as a result of that decision.

As a result of the goodwill that we built up in Washington, DC, we developed a much closer defence relationship with the United States. As a result of building up a closer defence relationship with the US, we expanded the geopolitical space for Singapore, and we have much more freedom of action than a small state can have on its own. And as we look ahead and as we think about how we defend ourselves in the long term, it pays to have this close defence relationship with the US. I can tell you that small states that ignore geopolitical realities, and assume that they can just take a moral stand and get away with it, are the states that get into trouble in the long run.

Chairperson: Ladies and gentlemen, I will now invite you to vote again to see whether or not your views have changed, by the other side particularly the Opposition, to change your mind. The motion is "Pragmatism should be retained as Singapore's governing philosophy". Those of you who agree, please press "1", those of you who disagree, please press "2".

2ND VOTING RESULT:
PROPOSITION — 56.4%, OPPOSITION — 43.6%

Chairperson: And we have your answers. Well done to the Opposition, very interesting. And we will open the floor to questions and see whether or not you manage to tilt the balance again. But before I do that, I will ask each team a question. For the Proposition, I would like to ask: Is pragmatism a philosophy or is it merely a means to an end?

Kishore Mahbubani: Pragmatism is actually a very deep philosophy that goes back a long, long time. There is even a school of philosophy called pragmatism. Over time, humanity accumulates wisdom. And as part of that wisdom, in order to succeed, to be able to deliver a good life for their citizens, to be able to ensure that people can escape wars, societies have developed this philosophy of pragmatism. If it were just a means to an end, then presumably you would say that anything goes. But I think you will notice that most of the philosophers who have argued in favour of pragmatism suggest that if your goal is to create a better life for your people, if your goal at the end of the day is to ensure that people are better off rather than worse off, then you should move towards pragmatism. And you will find roots of pragmatism in all of the great cultures in the world, not just in Western philosophy. You will find it in Indian philosophy and in Chinese philosophy. So it's something that is found all over the world, and the fact that it has existed in all cultures for such a long period of time suggests that it is a philosophy and not just a means to an end.

Chairperson: Thank you and now to the Opposition. Surely pragmatism remains important for the success of Singapore in the long run. How would you rate it compared to the other values and ideals that you think the government should consider in how it governs Singapore?

Eugene Tan: Certainly, pragmatism is important. I spoke earlier about the need for us to be even-handed — looking at what pragmatic considerations, what sort of moral objectives and what sort of aspirational concerns we can address. Let me give you an example. We all talk about how globalisation has enabled Singapore to prosper. But we also know that globalisation does not lift all boats to the same level. For a long time, we have worked on the premise that most people have benefitted from globalisation. This utilitarian perspective has worked very well for us. It is easy to justify as a matter of public policy. But things have changed. So now we have the Workfare Income Supplement. It is an attempt to recognise that economic globalisation does not benefit everyone. But as a society, we cannot just leave these people by the wayside. There is a need to try to help them level up. You can see the pragmatic consideration of wanting to be open to globalisation. But there is also the recognition that we need to be more than pragmatic. Madam Chair, it's not about preferring one over the other. It is really about being even-handed.

Chairperson: Vikram, would you like to add to that?

Vikram Khanna: We are not against pragmatism. Like I said, it is like motherhood. Nobody is against it. The problem is if you want to make it the sole ruling philosophy.

Chairperson: Or the most important ruling philosophy.

Vikram Khanna: No, that is not what the motion says. The motion says pragmatism should be the governing philosophy.

Chairperson: So are we now having a discussion on the motion?

Vikram Khanna: No, I do not want to be too technical. I mean, we also need a moral compass. We need principles. We need things that, as the Prime Minister said, are unshakeable. We don't have the rule of law because it's pragmatic. We have rule of law because it's intrinsically good in and of itself. We don't have meritocracy or interethnic harmony because it's pragmatic. It is good. I think we must have things that are intrinsically good in and of themselves whether they are pragmatic or not. I think that's the difference.

Chairperson: Thank you, Vikram. I'd like to now open the floor to questions. If you'd like to pose it to a particular member of the team, please let us know. Anybody? The gentleman over there in blue. Please identify yourself when you get to the microphone and whether or not you are opening the question to everyone, a team or to specific people.

Question 1: I'm Jared. My question is for all the speakers. We were talking about philosophy so I thought I'd take a page from Plato's *The Republic* and ask this. Pragmatism is a governing philosophy and it applies not just to states but perhaps to people too. You might say people have governing philosophies. So it seems to me that somebody whose governing philosophy is pragmatism might not be a very good person. As a child, I don't want my mum to be pragmatic to me. I want her to love me even though she might not get a good cost benefit return. I want her to love me even though she might take reputational damage. It should never be that kind of pragmatic consideration. And so, people should not always be pragmatic. So maybe we want to think that states also should not always be pragmatic, at least as a kind of governing philosophy. Does that sound right or is there some problem with the analogy between people and states? Or where have I gone wrong?

Chairperson: Jared, are you posing that question to anybody in particular?

Vikram Khanna: I will volunteer to answer. I think that is a very interesting question. I think it is true that pragmatism can also become a personal belief system. I do not know if you have seen the movie *Whatever Works* by Woody Allen. It is a fantastic movie. Let me summarise the plot. It is about a 70-something-year-old guy in New York called Boris Yellnikoff who has a very bleak view of life. He decides that he should just do whatever works to make him happy. And then every character in the film has the same philosophy. They just do whatever works. And so Boris gets married to a woman 50 years younger than he is and then divorces her. Her parents, who are from the south of the US and very religious, come to New York to rescue their daughter from this dirty old man. The mother, who is a strict Christian, decides to become an avant-garde photographer and has multiple boyfriends. The father, who is also religious, discovers that he is gay and that he can have a gay life in New York and so on. This is a comedy of course, this is Woody Allen, but I think it is very illustrative of what can happen when people adopt a philosophy of "whatever works" in their personal lives.

There is a guru of personal pragmatism in China called Ding Yuan Zhi who wrote a book called *Square and Round*. It offers pragmatic advice on how to live your life and there are some very interesting tips. For example, he says to show indifference to another person, release your handshake immediately on contact. If you want to make advances towards a certain lady, you should take advantage when she is sick; doing so will surely be effective because she will be weak and most in need of comfort. If you want to buy cheap clothes, ask the price of expensive clothes first. If you have a small request, first make a large request. Then let the other person refuse. When he feels apologetic, that is when you make your small request. So this is a pragmatic guru, his book is a perversion of an American self-help book.

Now this is the sort of behaviour that you will get when people make pragmatism a personal belief system and I think that is dangerous. I think it can happen. Most people are not like that. Most people believe in principles, in morality. And most people have a moral compass. So when you appeal to people, you have to show those qualities. You cannot say I am doing this because it's pragmatic. You sometimes have to say I am doing this because it is right.

Chairperson: Thank you, Vikram. Would anybody like to respond or say anything?

Tong Yee: I have two quick responses to this. First, I want to make sure that we do not detract from the motion here — it is about pragmatism being our governing philosophy. I think every single individual has every right to be whatever they choose to be and I have every right to be idealistic and I really am. I find it weird that I myself am sitting on this particular side of the debate. Second, we are not against what the Opposition is saying. You are saying that there needs to be some sort of balance and I absolutely get it. But the question is really whether pragmatism should be the governing philosophy.

Kishore Mahbubani: I must say that I love the story by Woody Allen. One of the great things about living in New York was the ability to watch a lot of Woody Allen movies. And people watch them and enjoy them; but to the best of my knowledge, very few people replicate what they see in Woody Allen movies in their personal lives. Also, that is not what this debate is about. It is not about what you do in your personal life. I would certainly agree that in your personal life, the most important and fundamental thing is to be moral and ethical and to do the right thing. That is the case in your personal life. But remember that nation states are different from human beings.

The tragedy of history — and there are five thousand years of human history you can go back and refer to — shows us that when states, especially small states, begin to behave like priests and saints, they end up in deep trouble. So that is not what we are debating today. We are not debating what you should do with your personal life. I completely support the Opposition when they say that we should not be pragmatic in our personal lives. But that is not what the debate is about. The debate is about what states should do and, more importantly, what small states should do. And when you come to the final round of voting, I hope you will remember that you are voting about states and not human beings.

Tong Yee: Let me put it this way. When I first chose to participate in this debate, I asked myself a question: "Why on earth would I agree to something insane?" I love Singapore deeply and I am very proud of it. And I am not in a position to say that I am proud of Singapore because we have been completely pragmatic. I think it has been a sound, realistic philosophy and, at the same time, we have been courageous. We have been bold and when we look at what we are debating about, I think we have something to be proud of. And I don't think that feeling of pride comes completely from a Machiavellian utilitarian approach. Singapore has balanced itself as well as we can. And as far as the state is concerned, yes, we have pragmatism as our governing philosophy. I don't think that we have lost all those other ideals or values that make us stand out as a very small and very proud nation.

Vikram Khanna: Kishore, I agree that we are talking about states and not about personal behaviour. We are only answering the gentleman's question. He asked about personal behaviour. That said, I do not think it is irrelevant. I think if a state exhibits 100 per cent pragmatism in everything it does, it can influence people's personal behaviour. It should not, but it can and it does in some cases.

Chairperson: Okay, I'd like to take back control of the debate and open it back to the floor. Are there any other questions? Yes, please.

Question 2: My question is directed at the Opposition. If I may suggest, if pragmatism is not to be our governing philosophy, then presumably the corollary to that is that ideology should be our governing philosophy. So let me posit you the case of Charlie Hebdo. Freedom of speech is an ideology. If ideology is to be a governing philosophy, then you should have complete freedom of speech under any circumstance. That is numero uno but then you wind up with Charlie Hebdo. A pragmatic view would say freedom of speech is a good thing but we need to temper it with what is practical and what is appropriate for society at large. And then you would say, maybe you would want to temper that ideology with a sense of what is real and practical in a multiracial society. So in that context do you really think that ideology should really trump pragmatism?

Vikram Khanna: I do not think we ever said we should throw out pragmatism and substitute it with ideology. Pragmatism must be there. Pragmatism should be an element of any governing philosophy. But it is not the whole thing, that is the point. The motion says pragmatism should be the governing philosophy, not a philosophy should be tempered by pragmatism. So I totally agree with you, you cannot take a black-and-white ideological view of the Charlie Hebdo issue.

But this is not just an issue of pragmatism versus ideology. It is also about values. Unbridled free speech is one of France's core values. In our case, free speech does not extend to having the freedom to insult someone's religion. We take this position not merely out of pragmatism, but because we believe it to be right in itself.

Eugene Tan: Do not be blindsided. Like it or not, pragmatism as it is practised in Singapore can operate, and does operate, as a form of ideology. It says let us focus on what works; it does not matter how we are going to get there. We should not be fooled by the Proposition's view that we are proposing an ideological stand. There will always be competing ideologies. What is important is that we have to be even-handed. Freedom of speech is as important in our society as the right of people to not be offended, particularly when it comes to their religious beliefs. And we are not saying that we should sacrifice one for the other. It is really approaching it in a contextual manner. So the text, take the Constitution for example, operates in a context. It's important to recognise that.

Chairperson: Thank you, Eugene. Would you like to say anything, Kishore?

Kishore Mahbubani: I think I understand why they got more votes in the second round. They seem to be agreeing with us more and more. I know that they are in a difficult position as they are arguing against motherhood but, you know, they are going all over the place. You either say that pragmatism should be retained as our governing philosophy or you say it should be dropped. The Opposition should be arguing that pragmatism should be dropped, but they are not doing so.

Chairperson: Thank you. The gentleman at the back, if you could just give us your name.

Question 3: I am Paul Tambyah from the medical school. My question is directed at Professor Mahbubani. You quoted Mr Rajaratnam. I would like to give you another quote from Mr Rajaratnam, who was famously quoted as saying Singaporeans should not become people who know the price of everything and the value of nothing. And, in fact, if you think about it, 50 years ago, we had world champion badminton players, we had a hockey team that went to the Olympics and did not get thrashed 16–1 by Malaysia, we had the centre of the Malay film industry and we had a dynamic rock 'n' roll culture. But all of those things were rejected because they were not pragmatic, because they did not help deal with the basic needs of Singapore society, which were housing, medical care and other development imperatives. As a result of which, we had to jettison our sporting and cultural icons at the altar of pragmatism.

So my question is when it comes to an issue like sovereignty, which we discussed in the morning, do we really have to sacrifice our principles in support of what our current American president calls a dumb war, a rash war, just so that we can achieve a certain amount of limited goals? I really believe — in line with what the Opposition is saying — that pragmatism itself has got very limited benefits. It is going to help you in the short term, it is going to help you achieve goals A and B. But if you want to have long-lasting goals, you need something bigger, better than that, and I think the audience here has gone from 73 to 56 and at the next step, they will vote for the Opposition. Thank you.

Kishore Mahbubani: I wish we had a supporter in the audience as strong as that! Three quick points. First, I completely agree with Mr Rajaratnam on what he said about individuals. It is wrong for individuals to know the price of everything and not the value of anything. And that is why I emphasised that, for individual behaviour, the most important thing is to be moral; I completely agree with Mr Rajaratnam there. I could not quite follow your second point about us losing the cultural icons because there is an echo effect up here (*on stage*). But let me emphasise that not all of the decisions that Singapore has made in the last 50 years have been correct. Like any other society, Singapore has made mistakes. To give you a large and obvious example, in our rush to develop and modernise, we did not preserve neighbourhoods like Chinatown. Beautiful old districts were torn down. But that was the price we paid for rapid development in the early days. So we made mistakes. The critical point is: if you are pragmatic, you learn from your mistakes; and that is what Singapore has been doing over the years. Now, finally, your point about the Iraq war. You are right. There are people who are opposed to it, and there are good reasons for opposing it. But the question is: what should Singapore, as a small state, do?

Chairperson: Thank you. Would either of you like to respond to that? If not, we'll open the floor to questions again.

Question 4: My name is Rahul and my question is for the Opposition. You are essentially arguing that pragmatism should not be our governing philosophy.

So then the question is, what should our governing philosophies be? I know you mentioned values and ideals but could you give specifics?

Vikram Khanna: I think I have mentioned in my brief remarks that we should have a pragmatic approach to our governing philosophy. That is completely different from saying pragmatism should be our governing philosophy. A pragmatic approach would include elements of pragmatism. Of course there are times when we have to be pragmatic. There are times when we also have to be moral. There are times when we have to take a stand on what is right and wrong. There are times when we have to have things that are unshakeable, things that have to be done whether they are pragmatic or not.

We have mentioned the rule of law, interethnic harmony and meritocracy. There are societies that have ditched these things. There are societies that have ditched the rule of law. The rule of law has become the rule of man, or some men. There are societies that do not practise tolerance towards all religions. There are also societies that practise ethnic majoritarianism. They do these things because they think it is pragmatic for them. That is not what Singapore should do. It would go against our core values. These values are part of our governing philosophy. So there are many elements of what our governing philosophy should contain. Pragmatism is one of them and only one of them.

Chairperson: Is there another question from the floor?

Question 5: My question to the Proposition is this. Could you please explain to Singapore citizens what the pragmatic value of the national pledge is? Because the layman on the street does not deeply believe that idealism should be the governing philosophy of the government. However, we need to implement idealism in a pragmatic way rather than the other way round. So I deeply believe that idealism should be our governing philosophy. Otherwise, if I propose to you, let us abolish the national pledge — because what is the pragmatic value for the layman on the street to recite the national pledge every National Day?

Chairperson: So the question is what is the practical purpose of reciting the pledge? What is the purpose of having a pledge?

Tong Yee: For me, it is entirely tied to context. If you are dealing with a multicultural and multireligious young nation, I think the national pledge is one of the most pragmatic things you will ever see. It talks about equal opportunity, it talks about the fact that we treat all people equal, and although a one nation itself is an ideal, it is pushing for a certain ideal. It is very pragmatic.

Chairperson: Over there, gentleman in the blue shirt.

Question 6: My name is Osman from Pertapis. Actually, I felt very connected with Professor Eugene Tan when he talked about the even-handed approach. To be seen as a caring government, the pragmatic approach is one good thing. But on the flipside, you could also be seen to adopt excessive or even extreme measures to achieve your pragmatic policies. So in 500 BC, Aristotelian ethics recommended the golden mean, which is prevalent in Islam, Christianity and Buddhism, where, for any policy, you have to take the middle mean between the extremes so that you will develop a caring and sharing society where nobody is left out. But if you keep on pursuing a very pragmatic approach on the flipside, you might be likely to be seen as oppressive or even sidelining certain communities or certain issues that are important to the minorities. I suggest that we adopt a pragmatic golden mean approach. What do you say, Professor Tan?

Chairperson: Professor Tan, please.

Eugene Tan: Thank you, Osman, for your support! Hopefully you can persuade people on your table to support us as well. I emphasised earlier the importance of being even-handed. We are not suggesting that we replace one ideology with another. But as society matures, we need to go beyond being pragmatic. It does not mean that pragmatism is thrown out of the window. It just means that pragmatism will now have to co-exist with other equally important things. Had we been pragmatic, well, we might as well not have the national pledge. The pledge exhorts us to do many things, and I think the Proposition has, in many ways, acknowledged the importance of not being pragmatic but to hold ourselves to a higher standard, to bring ourselves to a higher level. Is it "pragmatic" to do away with minorities? One could say that. I have students who have said that we should have an all-Chinese workforce in a company because it would be much easier to not have to cater for *halal* food during company events and the employees could all speak in Chinese or the same dialect. But is that what we want? Because this is what pragmatism will ultimately lead us to. We have got to go beyond that, recognising that pragmatism is essentially going for whatever works. It is important; we do not deny that. But we need to rise above that and recognise that we shouldn't be enslaved by pragmatism. Ultimately, we should ask ourselves, what is the point of Singapore being here? We might as well not exist at all *if* that is the "pragmatic" thing to do.

Chairperson: Does either of you have anything to say to him?

Kishore Mahbubani: I am somewhat confused by the arguments of the Opposition. The key line you used, Eugene, is that as society matures, we need to go beyond pragmatism. But go where? What is unclear about your argument is: where are you taking us? I know you keep saying that we should become more moral and choose ideals, but are you actually advocating that we abandon pragmatism? And if you are saying that we are not abandoning pragmatism, then aren't you agreeing with us? So what I am trying to say is, what are you disagreeing with? Are you saying that Singapore should drop pragmatism as its governing philosophy? And if we drop it, where do we go, what is your destination and where are you taking us?

Chairperson: You have to respond.

Eugene Tan: Thanks for the extra airtime. We certainly take the view that pragmatism must remain part of the governing philosophy. We recognise the importance that pragmatism plays in public policy having to deal with finite resources. But we need to go beyond that. We need to go beyond pragmatism because society demands more and it is also the right thing to do. If we say that we should do away with the poor, with minorities, on one level, it can be seen as pragmatic. On another level, it would go against what Singapore actually represents. Professor Kishore Mahbubani has been trying to press us to say what would come in place of pragmatism. We have offered the perspective that we should be even-handed. We should now have the even-handed approach, balancing pragmatism with what it means to be Singaporean, what it means to be in Singapore. What does our society stand for? I think that's important. If we want to have a soul as a nation, we need to go beyond cost-benefit analysis.

Kishore Mahbubani: Let me state an important historical fact which is important for us to take on board during this debate. The British left behind multiracial colonies in all parts of the world: Guyana in South America, Cyprus in Europe, Sri Lanka in South Asia, Singapore in South-east Asia and Fiji in the Pacific. If you look at this list of five, four out of the five failed to manage their ethnic relationships because the societies were not pragmatic. They took an ideological position, which then led to disaster. So if your concern is, say, ethnic harmony and making sure we all stay together, I suggest that you go and study these cases of the former British colonies, and study why they failed. The fundamental reason why they failed is because they were not pragmatic. So if your goal is to ensure that, then the rest should learn from Singapore.

Eugene Tan: I think Professor Mahbubani failed to mention that the British left behind a dominant race in all these other countries. We chose not to take that "pragmatic" path. The British decided in Malaya, in Sri Lanka, to have a dominant group. We decided to go against that and that has made all the difference. Because we chose not to be pragmatic, we chose to treat the minorities with sensitivity, short of affirmative action.

Chairperson: Would anybody else like to ask a question? Gillian, please.

Question 7: May I invite the speakers to engage in very specific policy issues. First, a choice was made to license two integrated resorts. Was that a pragmatic decision for job creation and do you stand against that? Another policy decision is that we made a choice to institute CPF [Central Provident Fund], which is to beat our human instincts not to plan for the future and force us to set aside money for retirement. Is that a pragmatic choice? Was it unwise? Third, we made a practical choice to institute GRCs [Group Representative Constituencies]. It is a basic minimum guarantee that minorities will have representation in parliament. Was that a pragmatic or incorrect choice? Finally, the government constantly makes the choice to have public consultation in-between general elections. It is a pragmatic and practical choice to engage as many people as possible as they make their policy choices. Is that a pragmatic choice but an incorrect and wrong one? So can the motion "the conference resolves that pragmatism remains important and should be retained as our government philosophy" be turned down?

Chairperson: Thank you, Gillian, for the four questions. I suggest we take them by theme. The first question was on the integrated resorts, the second was on CPF and choice, the third was on GRCs and the fourth on if it is correct for the government to have public consultation between general elections to engage as many people as possible in the last fifty years? So there were four questions in Gillian's one question. Would you all like to take all four at one go or I suggest we take it topic by topic. Can I suggest that we take the issue of the integrated resorts and the decision on the integrated resorts? Could I ask the Proposition to take that on first?

Tong Yee: Kishore is going to kill me for this one. If there is one thing that I can't do, it is speak against what I genuinely believe in. I understand the reasons why we opened the integrated resorts but that was something that we chose based on our pragmatic reasons and I personally am against them. I get that we have a prettier skyline right now but, in the social sector, we are dealing with a lot of people who have not benefitted from this. So personally, I would lean towards the other end. I really want to present it as an idea itself, that this is really perhaps one of the exceptional things that we did, but I think that it is still being debated.

Chairperson: So the Proposition would have rejected its own motion in this case because he does not believe that the government made a correct choice there?

Kishore Mahbubani: No, hang on. I think you have misstated what Tong Yee is trying to say. We did say earlier that the government has made mistakes in the process of pragmatism, and you can argue that the casinos were a big mistake. Frankly, in my case, to be completely blunt and honest with all of you, my father went to jail because of gambling debts. My family suffered because of gambling. So if you were to ask me if I would vote for casinos, my answer is no.

Chairperson: Would the Opposition like to take on that issue?

Vikram Khanna: I would concede yes. I think having casinos was a pragmatic decision: it is a job creator, it adds another engine to the economy and tourism, and it has been a success. While there have been problems and cases of problem gambling, there are safeguards to prevent that and I think the social fallout has not been that bad. So it was totally a pragmatic decision and I have no problem with it.

Eugene Tan: I think we have forgotten who the Proposition is and who the Opposition is! The IRs were a pragmatic decision. That is where many of us have difficulty because we feel that it goes against certain things that we believe in. Have we become bankrupt of ideas such that we need to have the IRs? Having said that, I think it's also important to recognise that we are also trying to square the circle. Singapore opted for the IRs for whatever pragmatic and economic considerations but we are also trying to see how we can create a virtue out of a vice. How can we come out with new forms of regulation that will ensure that the casinos and the IRs actually work for us? To some extent, we have done so. But there will always be that constant tension. This constant tension will help public policy to be better. If we had just been solely pragmatic, we would not have bothered about the social fallout that would have arisen from the introduction of casino gaming in Singapore. So I hope that sets clear that we are the Opposition!

Chairperson: In the interest of time, I'm going to focus on the next question regarding GRCs before we have the closing arguments. So if I could ask the Proposition to take on the issue of GRCs.

Kishore Mahbubani: Actually, I am glad Gillian asked the question about GRCs because I want to emphasise that the word "our", in this case, refers to Singapore as a society and not the ruling party. So we do not have to argue in favour of what the ruling party does. The GRCs were a decision made by a political party, and not necessarily a decision by Singapore as a society.

Eugene Tan: This is where Professor Mahbubani has revealed the soft underbelly of pragmatism. We are not clear, in the end, to what ends, or rather who, does pragmatism serve. Sometimes, we are not clear whether it even serves the people. Sometimes, we are not clear whether it serves the government and, sometimes, we are not clear whether it serves the state. Looking at Professor Mahbubani's response, it is clear that there are difficulties with pragmatism as it is practised because it could easily be used to further the ends of the ruling party. It could certainly be used to further the ends of society. So what I am saying is that this is a very fungible concept. It is as much an ideology that enables the ruling party — the government — to use it, and to say that it works for society and that is why we should have it. So in response to Gillian, I would say that the GRC scheme was a pragmatic response to the government's claim then that people were voting along racial lines. But I see also the idealism that is also vested in it. The idealism is to have the political parties behave in a moderate manner. In order to win votes, they need to pool votes from the different racial groups. That represents both a pragmatic response as well as an idealistic response. As I tell students in my constitutional law class, let's look at the policies, the institutions for what they are worth. Let us, for the moment, put aside how the ruling party uses it to its advantage. But it still raises the real possibility that pragmatism can be misused.

Chairperson: Thank you. Vikram?

Vikram Khanna: Just to add to the point of pragmatism for whom. I think the issue that Eugene has mentioned is very important. There are many questions here where it is not clear. I mean you might say yes, it should be pragmatism for society. But let me give you two small concrete examples. Singapore has the highest acreage of golf courses among any country in the world. Who is this pragmatic for? Who does it work for? If all Singaporeans were golfers, I would say yes, build more golf courses. But I think if 2 per cent are golfers, who does it work for? Another thing, this goes back to history a little bit. We incarcerated many artists and playwrights in the 1970s. We had Operation Spectrum in 1987 when more people were incarcerated. This served to stifle artistic and cultural expression. Was this pragmatic? Who was this pragmatic for? Was it pragmatic for society? I am not going to answer this question. I will leave it to you to decide. So there are a lot of things that we have done which are of questionable value and I would not say they were quite so pragmatic.

Chairperson: I'd like to now invite the teams to make their closing arguments. For the Opposition, Eugene please, if you can take the standing microphone. You have five minutes.

Eugene Tan: Madam Chair, ladies and gentlemen, the Proposition has tried to paint Vikram and me as the high priests of idealism. Far from it. I would put it to you that there would have been no Singapore of today had pragmatism not prevailed in 1965. We would have simply keeled over and adopted the different courses that Mr Janadas Devan outlined earlier. My team's stand is that pragmatism remains undoubtedly important. What we have tried to do is to show how even in the different policies that may have come across as being pragmatic, idealism, values and principles have been nurtured in them as well. Being pragmatic is a given. But we must learn to leaven it even more. Pragmatism, because it focuses on what works, would also mean that we forget that we do have choices, even if they are difficult choices. It is important, as we move ahead, that we recognise that we do have a choice.

Pragmatism, unfortunately, tends to curtail any discussion because it gets people to focus only on whatever works. Pragmatism would be wholly inadequate in our next lap. In fact, it would probably be the recipe for our downfall. As I said earlier, it can get us through the day but we need more than pragmatism to get us through the night. In his book *Drive*, Daniel Pink reminds us of how motivation is intrinsically powered, comprising three elements: autonomy, which is the desire to be self-directed; mastery, which is the urge to be better, to excel; and third, purpose, the yearning to be part of something larger than ourselves.

As you can see, pragmatism will not enable us to rise above ourselves. It will suppress whatever autonomy we want because we will all have to worship at the altar of pragmatism. It will not encourage us to adopt a craftsman-like attitude, to attain mastery in whatever we do. Instead it will encourage us to go for what is expedient, what is convenient and to take short cuts. We must continue to have that sense of mission. But pragmatism enervates that very sense of mission.

Second, the Proposition has tried to paint the motion as being about society and not about individuals. But isn't it individuals who make up a society? And it is important here to recognise how the state's approach to many issues can ultimately affect how Singaporeans view policies. This is where it can be very problematic for nation-building in Singapore because pragmatism encourages citizens to take a very transactionary approach. What is in it for me? That results in the legitimacy of government policy being measured in pragmatic terms and, very often, that means in economic terms. That is why we now have this overwhelming preference for value rather than values.

Look at housing, for example. It is not only something that we think of, it is something that we think with. Think about how the Singaporean male has been caricatured. When he wants to get married to the lady he loves, he will say, "Let us go and apply for a HDB flat". It's all about using housing to think about these things.

Third, the Proposition asked where pragmatism would take us. I think it will enervate us of our ability to govern; it will take away the energy for collective action because we will tend to think about what works for us individually. So is it any surprise that, on economic matters, people are not really taking action in any meaningful way because they are constantly reminded that those are the issues that they are very worried about? It is easy to say that we do make mistakes and that pragmatism cannot be blamed. But it reminds us that pragmatism also consigns us into thinking only in terms of trade-offs. We need to go beyond trade-offs. So let me conclude: we do have a choice, and we should stop worshipping at the altar of pragmatism.

Chairperson: Thank you, Eugene. I'd like to now invite Kishore to present his closing remarks for the Proposition.

Kishore Mahbubani: My partner Tong Yee began by saying that as someone from the NGO world, it was a very unpragmatic decision on his part to come and argue in favour of pragmatism. I made an equally unpragmatic decision because I arrived this morning at 6am from Davos, where I fell ill, so you can see that I am slightly incapacitated in this debate. But when Janadas pushed me very hard to take this role, I actually agreed because it reflects a genuine and deep personal worry that I have about Singapore. I do worry when I hear Eugene say that it is time for us to go beyond pragmatism and weigh in other factors. There is a huge danger in his statement because there is one fundamental fact about Singapore that has not changed; that one fundamental fact is that we remain a small state. And fortunately, we have several thousand years of human history to go back and study in order to understand the state of small states. And clearly, the lessons of history teach us that when small states — and I must emphasise that we are talking about the state and not the government — stop being pragmatic, they get into deep trouble. I can predict three concrete examples of big challenges that are coming our way.

Number one is geopolitical. There is going to be an enormous geopolitical contest between the United States and China; I guarantee it. And if Singapore does not react carefully and pragmatically to this great geopolitical divide, we will suffer. Do not try to be moralistic in geopolitics if you are a small state because your head will be cut off. And that has not changed.

In the area of the economy, we know, even some of the leading developed states are struggling to cope with the new forces of globalisation. We have to change and adapt very quickly if we are going to make it, and if we stop being nimble and pragmatic, I assure you that Singapore will be washed away very quickly by another wave of global competition.

And finally, to refer to the internal area of society, which is what our opposition has focused on, we still remain a multiracial state. That has not changed. And I am glad that Piyush Gupta brought up the issue of the Charlie Hebdo affair. Because if you take the non-pragmatic approach, and you take the ideological approach that freedom of speech is everything that matters, Singapore is finished. As I was flying back this morning, I read an editorial in the *Economist* about the Charlie Hebdo affair that was pure rubbish. And if we follow that rubbish, we will suffer as a consequence. So as you can see, in all the big challenges that are coming our way, if we are to preserve Singapore as it is, we have to remain pragmatic. Now the key word that the Opposition used was "ideals". I suggest to all of you that the highest ideal that we as fellow Singaporeans can have is to try and preserve this small island city-state, which has a land territory that is so absurdly small that it is smaller than a small island in a lake in Sumatra. And on that tiny bit of territory, you are trying to create a complex city state that is competing with the rest of the world, that is trying to surpass the rest of the world, and if you forget that you have so few resources and so little territory, and you take idealistic and moral positions, as our opposition is suggesting, then sadly Singapore will be finished. So please, I beg you, retain pragmatism as our governing philosophy.

Chairperson: Thank you very much, Kishore. Thank you, ladies and gentlemen. And it's now my pleasure to invite all of you to see whether your minds have been changed again by our speakers and to take the last vote for the day. The poll says pragmatism should be retained as Singapore's governing philosophy. Those of you who agree, please press "1" and send it in. Those of you who disagree, press "2" and send it in. So one thing we all found in common is that Mr Janadas Devan had huge persuasive powers on all of us.

3RD VOTING RESULT:
PROPOSITION — 63%, OPPOSITION — 37%

The vote has swung back somewhat. Sixty-three per cent for the motion and 37 per cent against the motion. Congratulations to both teams. I believe many of you, I hope many of you, found this to be interesting, learnt something from today's discussion and debate, and found it scintillating. I would have liked to see somebody argue that the Singapore government is idealistic, is an ideological party and is formed as an ideological party but it is pragmatic in the way it delivered its policy to achieve those ideological outcomes which are meritocracy, multiracialism, nuclear family, subsidised healthcare and education. That's just one way we could have argued but thank you all very much. I hope you all have a good rest of the conference.

4

Inter-Generational Ministerial Dialogue

CHAPTER 6

Dialogue with Deputy Prime Minister Teo Chee Hean and Minister Chan Chun Sing

Singapore Perspectives 2015 concluded with a dialogue session with Deputy Prime Minister (DPM) Teo Chee Hean and then-Minister for Social and Family Development Chan Chun Sing.[1] Chaired by IPS Director Janadas Devan, the dialogue session elicited a wide range of questions, including ones on national identity, welfare policies, immigration, ageing population and increasing political diversity in society. The following is a transcript of the dialogue.

Question: DPM, there has been a lot of discussion lately about the role of history in the formation of Singapore's national identity. You were only 11 years old when Singapore became independent. Did you personally expect Singapore to grow up so fast and have the luxury of debating questions about national identity? What about those early years of Singapore which made this historical assertiveness possible? In other words, how was the groundwork laid for what Singapore is today? In the same way, could I ask Minister Chan to provide a different age perspective on what formative influences and ideas gave you hope that this country would cohere. Sirs, questions for both of you, please.

---

[1] On 8 April 2015, the National Trades Union Congress (NTUC) Central Committee unanimously elected Minister Chan to be NTUC Secretary-General from 4 May 2015 to help strengthen labour leadership at NTUC and the link between the Labour Movement and the Government.

DPM Teo: As an eleven-year-old, my thoughts of what a nation would be were probably not well formed. But it was interesting to have lived through this period. I still remember going to the theatre and having to stand up when "God Save the Queen" was played at the start of every movie. I went to a Chinese kindergarten for one year. I studied in an English school but I studied both Malay and Chinese language when I was in Primary One and Two. When I was in Primary Three, my father had to decide if I would study Malay or Chinese. That was the momentous year of 1963. My father decided that I would study the Malay language. [Living through these events] was not something that I regretted. Rather, these were precisely the kinds of things that affect your identity as you go through life.

In secondary school, because I took Malay as a second language, I would go to Empat PM (Persatuan Persuratan Pemuda Pemudi Melayu, or 4PM) in Jalan Eunos to take part in Malay oratorical contests. These experiences provided me with formative ideas that shaped the way I thought about Singapore and Singaporeans. I used to have conversations with my late grandmother, who was born in 1902. When we talked about social attitudes, she would say in Teochew, "*nang deng nang* [we Chinese]," and I would say "no, *nang* Singapore *nang* [we Singaporeans]". She probably thought I was being rude to her. But these were the differences in social attitudes and the way we thought about ourselves as we progressed.

1966 was the first year we recited the pledge. Radio and Television Singapore came to our school to film students taking the pledge. As the head prefect, I raised the flag every day. I was on television every morning and every evening when the national anthem was played. Watching myself raise the flag had a profound impact on my sense of national identity.

The defining experiences of national service also shaped my thoughts about race. When I was an NCC [National Cadet Corps] cadet, we did not have enough water bottles to go around. You will probably be horrified by this idea but when we went to field camp, we used to share water bottles. My Indian buddy and I would share a water bottle. He took a drink whenever he needed one and I took a drink whenever I needed one. We thought nothing of it. That was a defining experience in itself.

When I went to the UK to study, it was the first time I went anywhere further than Penang. I was 19 years old then. Being away from home somehow made me feel even more attached to Singapore and what Singapore is. I had a sense that there was something here that was special and there was something that I wanted to do.

So what were the fundamentals that helped us shape what we are today? I understand that you had a big debate [earlier today] on pragmatism. Pragmatism certainly had a lot to do with it but because of the cauldron of crisis from which we came, there was a sense that if we did not get this right we would be finished. There was a consensus that we needed to do things together. Each of us, regardless of our race and religion, had to invest something to create Singapore and not just fight for our own factional and sectoral interests. The good charismatic leadership of Mr Lee Kuan Yew and his team helped to point out and set the direction. They also gave us those fundamentals that are still true today: meritocracy, multiracialism, incorruptibility and self-reliance. Those are as much a part of our national identity and character, as are many of the other aspects. This is not a specific answer but an impressionistic answer based on my own experiences growing up in that period up to about the mid-1980s. This is perhaps a good time to hand over to Chun Sing.

Minister Chan: Thank you, DPM. I was born in 1969, just after the race riots. Of course, when I was born, I could not have known that the race riots had happened just one month before my birth. My formative experiences were slightly different from those of DPM. By the time I was born, everyone was calling themselves Singaporeans. The idea that we are all Singaporeans felt natural to almost everyone. But there were a few episodes that triggered me to think and ask myself, what does it mean to be a Singaporean and what does our national identity really mean? There were a couple of incidents that shaped my thinking.

I majored in Economics and Politics at Cambridge. I also read History. During the course of my studies, I began to wonder when we started calling ourselves "Singaporeans". Looking back, there was not really a time in the last 500 to 600 years when this place was independent. It was always a part of some larger entity — we were a part of Malaya, and prior to that we were a part of the British Empire. We were occupied by the Japanese and before the British came we were probably part of some sultanate from Johor to Malacca. We were also part of the Srivijaya Empire and the Majapahit Empire. It is quite odd and rare for us to be in this unique moment of history where we are independent.

In the military, we tend to think that since I am a Singaporean, everybody must accept that Singapore is an independent country and people should know that I am from an independent country. A senior military commander from one of the established armed forces around the world who was in charge of this region thought that the people of Singapore were called "Singaporees".

When I went to Indonesia as an army attaché, I began to realise how small we are as a country compared to Indonesia. A regional commander in East Java, Indonesia, asked me, "Why do you want to come to see me? Where is this place called Singapore? Oh, you happen to be in the southern part of Malaysia. Oh, I see. Malaysia is quite small compared to my province." During some of these moments, you begin to reflect and think that maybe we are quite unique as a country and we have defied the odds because of our pragmatism. We desire to remain independent but it is not easy because there is a price attached to it that not everyone wants to pay.

The freedom fighters in Papua Province in Indonesia once told me that they wanted to be independent. I asked them why. They could not really articulate it. More importantly, they were not really able to say whether they were prepared to pay the price of being independent, which meant having their own defence, foreign policies and economic strategies. On hindsight, the desire to be independent is unique, which defines our experience of trying to be a nation.

But we are now at a crossroads. The concept of national identity has two dimensions that are not mutually exclusive. Most countries in the world define their identity in exclusive terms — me versus you. This definition of national identity is backward-looking as it is based on speaking the same language, having the same race and religion and, for some, living in the same geographical area. There are some merits to this exclusive concept and some ease of building a sense of identity from this. But this exclusiveness also has its dangers. People become parochial and are unable to accept new ideas. They tend to be more backward-looking and this is the weakness of the concept.

But there is also a forward-looking concept that people build their identity on. It posits that although we are of different races, languages and religions, we share common ideals about how our society should be run, and which system of governance and values should define us. For example, we want to be an incorruptible and multiracial society. If we look around the world, very few countries define their national identity in just a backward-looking and exclusive way. They often include a forward-looking and inclusive way.

Our challenge going forward in the next era is to find that balance. We need something of the past to anchor us. The collective experiences that we have gone through — fighting for our country's independence, surviving as a small country, the SARS, economic crises and other incidents — have bonded us together as a nation. But going forward, we need to ask ourselves, what is the set of ideals that will help unite us, provide fresh perspectives and new energies? If we can find that balance between the two, then I am very confident that going forward we will have a very strong sense of what it means to be a Singaporean.

Question: Ministers, what are your thoughts on the recent measures to strengthen our social security system and provide more welfare benefits? Is this another pragmatic move or a populist one?

Minister Chan: I think it is a false dichotomy to say that we are either pragmatic or idealistic. You cannot be pragmatic without any ideals to guide you and you cannot expect things to happen if you are not pragmatic.

Let us take social policies as an example. As a country, our goal has always been to take care of everyone, regardless of race, language and religion. We strive to make sure we uplift those with the least. That is our ideal. The question is, how do we uplift those with the least? One of the guiding philosophies in my ministry is that we will try to do the most for those with the least. If I were to poll the audience here, would everyone agree with me that in trying to uplift everybody in society, we should try to do the most for the least? Would anybody disagree with this as an ideal? No? Maybe I should ask this in another way. How many of you agree to do the most for the least? Does everyone agree to do so?

So we all agree that we should do the most for those with the least. This is the easy part. The question becomes tricky when you try to implement policies, and have to answer questions, such as, what do you mean by doing more and who are those with the least? Here is an example from the early childhood sector. We used to provide a universal subsidy of S$300 to help families defray the costs of early childhood services. In the last few years, we have moved away from this and towards more targeted policies whereby the poorest families — those with a household income of less than S$1,000 — can obtain early childhood services for less than S$3 per child per month. The community will often raise money to cover that subsidy for most of the families.

Some of you might ask, why not provide early childhood services for free? This is because we want every family to have a sense of ownership and responsibility. It is not good as a policy and practice to take away people's dignity and pride and their sense of ability. So we put in place a token sum. To do the most for those with the least, we will focus on using resources for the last 10 to 20 per cent. Over time, we will give a bit less help to those on a higher income. All those who were for that philosophy and idealism just now would agree with me that this is the way to do things, right?

However, when the policy was announced, only a few people agreed that this is a good initiative. In fact, many people who earn S$7,501 a month [the income point at which subsidies were reduced] went to my Facebook page and said, "Why did I not get a higher subsidy than my neighbour?" Some of those who had received a few hundred dollars in subsidies were initially happy until they saw their neighbour getting a few hundred dollars more than them.

Now this goes to the heart of our challenges. We know what the correct thing to do is — to do the most for the least. But executing it is not so straightforward because we have to contend with human dynamics, and it is very difficult to do this. Many believe that they should get more help. But many who ask for more help sometimes forget that they are already getting quite a bit of help. There are also those who are getting help, but need much more. But if everyone fights only for his or her interests, then we would return to the system where we pretend to help everyone equally but end up helping nobody. So this is something we have to grapple with.

To live up to our ideal of doing more for those with the least, we need to ask ourselves honestly if we are one of those with less and therefore need more from society. If we can come to a nice social compact and understanding of this, I think we will be much stronger and our finite resources will be better targeted at those who need it most.

DPM Teo: The idea that it is time to start looking after the welfare of those who are less well off presupposes that we have not been doing so at all. In fact, many of the policies implemented since independence, from health, education to housing, have always been directed at uplifting Singaporeans, especially those with the least. When I was born, the life expectancy for males was around 59 years. This is of some significance to me, as I just turned 60 last year. Today, it is over 80. In terms of housing, people were living in overcrowded shanties without sanitation. I grew up in a reasonably comfortable home but it was served by the bucket system. Education used to be only for a privileged few. Today, education is available to everyone, including those with disabilities. These are important social policies that have uplifted masses of Singaporeans. They have accomplished social changes in ways that many countries have failed to do. Hence, when we talk about income inequality, we have to look back at our past and remember our accomplishments.

There is another perspective that I would like to point out. We are now adjusting some of our policies because society has changed. Ageing was not a major issue before but today a very large proportion of Singaporeans are going to be over the age of 65, many over 80. The fastest-growing segment is those who live, or will live, alone, largely because their children have their own homes. There is a large proportion of elderly Singaporeans who may be single. Their spouse may have passed away or their children may have flown the nest. We have had to readjust some of our health policies to take care of this group. Hence, we have the Pioneer Generation Package to take care of the pioneers and recognise their contributions to society. But the Pioneer Generation Package also addresses a very real need and concern that they have, which is healthcare.

MediShield Life will cover everyone for life, including those with pre-existing conditions. But the design of MediShield Life has to be sustainable. Many European countries have had to cut back on overly-generous welfare systems because they have not given enough emphasis on earning the dollar before spending it. A number of these countries are now experiencing very serious crises. It is important that you are able to keep the promise you made. Otherwise, you are writing a cheque drawing on somebody else's account. That is not a promise. The worst promise to make is when you write a cheque drawing on your children's account — on money that they have not earned yet. We want to avoid doing this by ensuring that the programmes and policies we put in place are sustainable.

In addition, it is not the amount spent on redistribution, but what it is spent on. You can spend a lot of money on, for example, providing rental housing for those who have no homes. But we have decided to spend the money on very large housing subsidies to help people own their own homes. This policy has an entirely different effect on inclusiveness, a sense of ownership and belonging to Singapore. We do not have unemployment benefits but we have Workfare and skills training. These have much more important long-term effects on the earning capabilities and self-dignity of individuals. So, it is not the extent of the redistribution but how you do it and whether you are able to sustain it in the long term without signing cheques using your children's accounts.

Minister Chan: Many tend to focus on the spending required for transfers from the highest to the lowest income tier. That is merely one dimension. If you look at what we have been doing over the last few years, the focus has not been on the amount transferred. That is the easy part. The focus has been on measures to help the low-income earners uplift themselves, and programmes to help the middle-income earners keep pace in the global competition. I do not know if you have been keeping track of Channel NewsAsia's series *Don't Call Us Poor*, but if you have, you would know that some of the challenges faced by those at that end of the spectrum are multifaceted and very complex. Giving out financial assistance may not resolve their problems.

Very often in our next lap of social services, we will have to emphasise helping people to be independent. We will have to mobilise volunteers who contribute their time and talent to support these families. Their lack of money is only a symptom. Their challenges often arise from being unable to invest in their children's education, provide a positive role model and a stable home environment for their children, and plan their finances. These problems may have a knock-on effect on the next generation.

In the next lap, we need to look beyond the transfer. The transfer has been able to uplift the broad middle. The families at the end of the income spectrum that MSF [Ministry of Social and Family Development] is most concerned will require more intensive intervention. I am very happy that the Pioneer Generation Package was not a promise on the future generation's ability to pay. We locked up all we think we need to finance the package for the rest of the years.

Question: Minister Chan, you mentioned that the monies required to fund the Pioneer Generation package have already been set aside. Will the package be extended to others? Is it not politically tenable to extend it to others, especially in the future?

Minister Chan: This is a question raised frequently by many of my residents, "When will I become the next pioneer generation?" Frankly speaking, we also hope to be able to offer a second Pioneer Generation package. But this is premised on a few factors: Do we have the means to do so? Will our society continue to share the belief that we should honour those who are old and have contributed to the making of Singapore? You must have the means and the will. Do you have a good government that can muster the resources and mobilise public opinion to do this? It is easy to promise, but will we actually be able to deliver? It depends on a few factors: first, the capabilities of the government; second, the capabilities of society; third, the willingness of our society to do so.

More importantly, how can we avoid the situation whereby government policies, particularly government subsidies, are turned into an auction in an election? This has happened in many countries all over the world. In trying to get elected, somebody will stand up and say, "I promise more than the next guy." After a while, the whole system unravels. This is unfortunately one of the challenges of any political system. It is always easy for someone to do one-upmanship and say, "I will promise more".

The only way to avoid this situation is to have an enlightened electorate. When someone promises to do more, you have to ask him how he will balance the books and how he will achieve his promises. These are tough questions. But it is the responsibility of any political party that promises to do more to explain the ways and magnitude in which they are going to distribute the subsidies.

So you are right. Today, we honour those who are 65 and above. It is easy for someone to say I will move it to 60 and give even more. The question is, how will this be done? We want to be in a happy situation to uplift our people and do much more. But that must go back to our ability to do so and our collective will to do so. We must also ensure that our attention and resources will be invested in those who require the most help. We must not turn the provision of subsidies into an auction.

DPM Teo: Just one personal note here, as someone who also missed the Pioneer Generation Package by just a few years, we hope that the next Cabinet will come to the right decision [laughs].... "You know what to do if you want my vote".

Minister Chan: It is not that far-fetched. There are many countries in the world today where the electoral politics are divided between different generations. Some people say that my generation will outvote yours. So I think this is something we have to be very careful with.

Question: Minister Chan, one difficult choice that we had to make in the past two years was about Singapore's population. While many people who spoke up said they would like to see a trimming of the numbers of foreign workers in Singapore, I'm not sure many people talked about how to do it. While the government proposes a halving of that number, the government also proposed a doubling of the historic productivity rate. So how do we get to the point where we have that enlightened citizenry you talked about, especially as we see political pluralism grow?

DPM, in the first session today, Ambassador Bilahari Kausikan said that for Singapore as a small state to make its way in the world, it has to be extraordinary. And to be extraordinary and relevant, we must have success in what we do and certainly that includes economic success. As you, Sir, also chair the productivity council, what are the difficult dilemmas that you face — workers, businesses, government, strategic choices — which will then have to be overcome this year, and going forward, in order to make that transition to a low-growth through high-base economy with half of what it had in terms of worker-growth rates but still be happily thriving and have enough money set aside so that you can have a Pioneer Generation Package when your time comes?

Minister Chan: The population issue is not something that is easy to communicate to the mass public because there are many dimensions to it and it involves long-term implications. Every society would obviously aspire to keep its society unique by having its own sense of identity. Every society would obviously feel a bit uneasy if the number of foreigners amongst them is too high. That is from the social perspective.

From the hard economics perspective, Singapore has 3.5 million citizens with a two plus million-strong workforce. We have to compete with some of the mega cities around the world with that number. A typical megalopolis like Beijing, Shanghai, Tokyo or Yokohama has about 20 million people as a conurbation. That is about 10 times our size. There is another unique thing about those cities compared to ours. People rotate in and out of big cities with a large hinterland. Those economically active individuals often rotate into the cities and the less economically active people rotate out of the cities. Among their population of 20 million, the proportion of economically active people is very high. That is the nature of global cities. They attract people who are energetic and dynamic. After making their fortunes in the cities, these people may rotate out. As a city state, we do not have that option. Our 2.5 million economically active people must take care of that 3.5 million. Whether you move to Changi, Jurong or Woodlands, you are still in Singapore.

The question is, how do we compete to make ourselves relevant to the rest of the world to earn a living? It is not an easy question to answer. There will be new industries. We bring them in because we want to provide new opportunities for our younger generation who would otherwise take over the jobs of the previous generation. They will earn the pay and salaries of the previous generation and compete in what we call the "Red Ocean of the Last Generation". The challenge is to stay competitive globally.

The second reason as to why we need foreigners is that we need skills to compete — although that is not a desired outcome and we would rather compete on quality than on price or skill. The question is, how can we encourage our 2.5-million workforce to be very productive? Theoretically, we should compete based on the quality of our ideas rather than the quantity of our inputs or the price of our products, but translating it into practice is not easy. Even if we have to turn into a new high-wage economy, it will take time for the industries to make this transformation.

This is why we have been going on and on about having to raise our productivity. We will continue to say this because to uplift the salaries and wages of our workers, we need to improve our productivity. In order to be more productive than other people who have more labour, land and resources than us, we need to invest in our workers. We have no other options. To create a niche as part of the global value-added chain, you need to be of a certain size.

The question is, can we do that with a two-point-something million population? It is not impossible, but I know that it is very difficult.

You can see that it is very difficult for other economies, even those with a hinterland, to provide opportunities for their younger generations. If we cannot provide opportunities for our younger generation, we might inadvertently trigger a cascading effect. The best and brightest in our society might decide to go elsewhere to seek their fortunes. However, when they see the world as their oyster, would they come back and call Singapore home? Or will we end up like some places with very good schools that bring up talented people who get absorbed by other cities? We will become a satellite revolving that mega conurbation. That would be quite sad for us.

So I think we have to strike a balance between bringing in some people who will add to Team Singapore and being able to assimilate them. As I mentioned, to shape our identity, we also need that balance between exclusivity, which is backward-looking, and inclusivity, which is forward-looking. If we can do that well, we can strengthen Team Singapore for the years to come. But this is a challenge that will continue as long as we are Singapore, that little red dot. It is our fate that, despite our finite natural resources, we have to compete in this hyper-competitive economy.

DPM Teo: Maybe I can make some comments about population and then talk about productivity.

Figure 1 shows how we are ageing as a population. The left shows where we are roughly today. The rows in blue are the males; the red rows indicate the females. Categorised by age groups in five-year bands. This is what we look like today: the baby boomers are just below that green line there, which is roughly the 60- to 65-year olds and that includes people like me who are going to go beyond 65 in the next five to ten years. There is a mini boom at around the 20-plus mark and that is the mini baby boom between the 1988 dragon year until 1997, after which births fell off again. If you look at the chart on the right-hand side, that is the picture of 2050 without immigration. It is top-heavy with a small base of younger people to support everyone.

Figure 2 shows that if we have no immigration by 2025, the Singapore citizen population will start to decline. It is a fate that is befalling Japan today, where you have an older population and the population has already started to decline. One of the more interesting statistics that I got from Japan is that more adult diapers are sold than baby diapers. That is quite a startling statistic.

Figure 3 is what is actually happening with our citizen workforce. Now this is a snapshot from 2030. The left vertical line shows the number of people coming into the workforce at around the age of 20 to 25, and the right vertical line shows the number of people leaving the workforce in 2030 at around age 65. You can see that the right-hand line is a lot higher than the left line (by 2030).

Figure 1 How our population is getting older

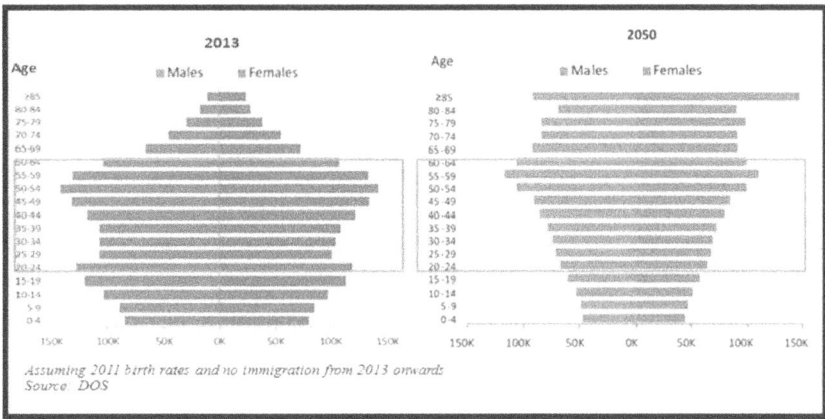

Figure 2 How our citizen population may shrink from 2025

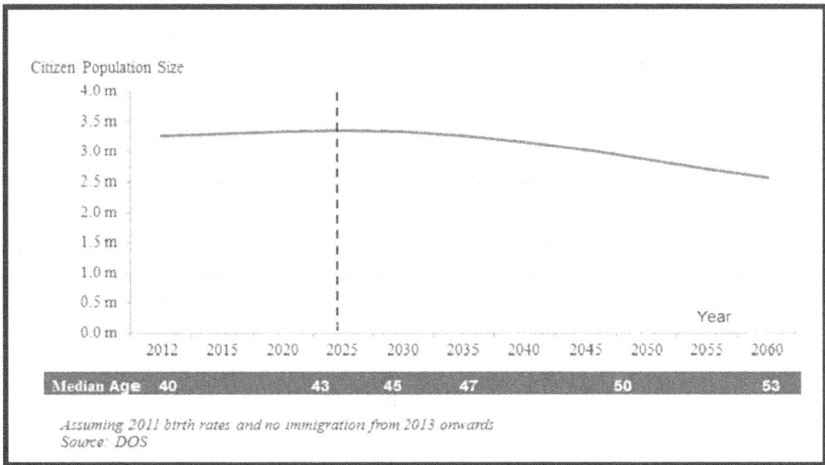

Figure 3 The current state of our citizen workforce

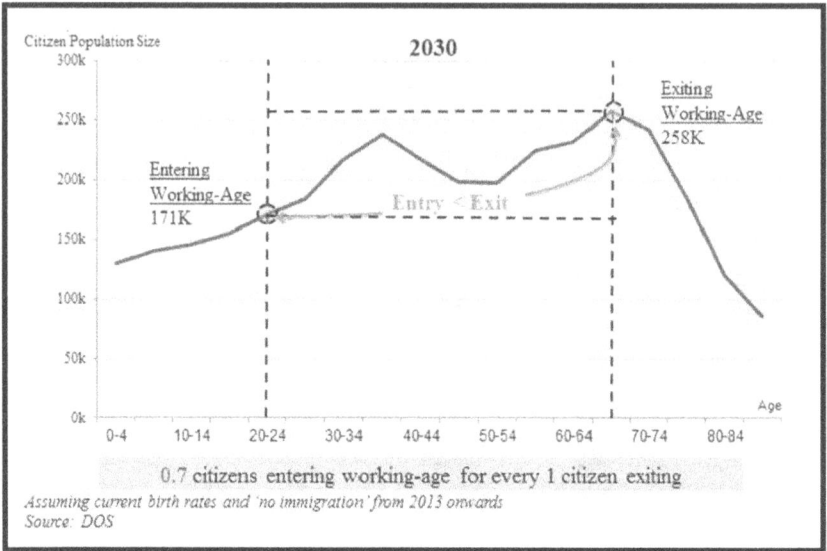

Prior to this, we were in a situation where the number of citizens leaving the workforce was smaller than the number of citizens entering the workforce.

Figure 4 shows how, in 1970, there were 13 citizens of roughly working age, namely, 20 to 64, to each citizen over the age of 65. Today, we have about 5.2. By 2030, with no immigration, the figure would be 2.1. These are quite startling statistics. It is all predetermined because we cannot wind the clock back and go back 16, 17, 18 years to produce the babies for now. So, this is where we are today. Therefore, we have to devise a strategy for moving forward.

Fortunately, we are a multicultural society that is immigrant-based. We drew our population from the great Asian civilisations and have been doing so for many years. But we still face friction in society. Imagine the amount of friction if monocultural societies such as China or Japan were to do that. They find it difficult to bring in people and add to the population without changing the core elements of their society. As an inherently multicultural and immigrant society, we have a better chance at addressing some of these issues, such as the declining fertility rate, through supplementing with immigration.

Figure 4   Proportion of working-age citizens to those 65 and above

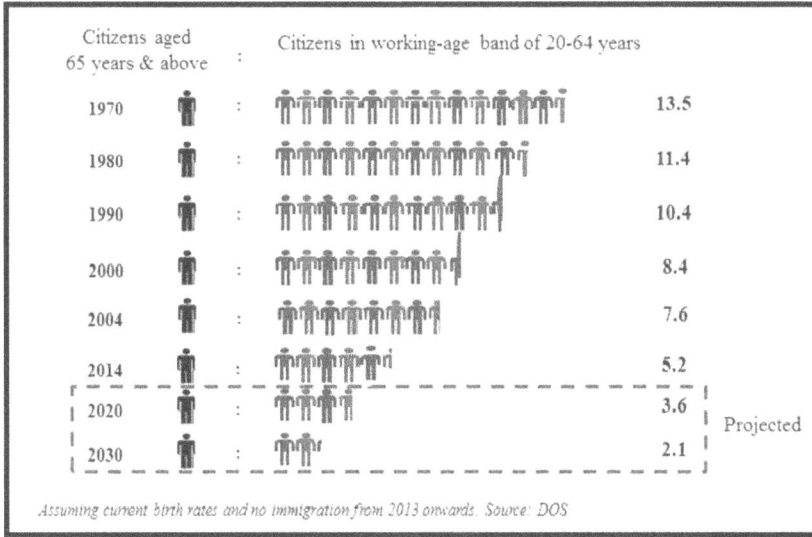

Citizens aged 65 years & above	:	Citizens in working-age band of 20-64 years		
1970	:		13.5	
1980	:		11.4	
1990	:		10.4	
2000	:		8.4	
2004	:		7.6	
2014	:		5.2	
2020	:		3.6	Projected
2030	:		2.1	

Assuming current birth rates and no immigration from 2013 onwards. Source: DOS

Our fertility rate is at 1.2. This means that a hundred people in this generation will result in 60 people in the next, and 36 in the generation after that. We simply need to be able to make up for the numbers that we lack. We are trying to increase our population by encouraging parenthood and marriage as much as possible. I see many more three-child families and have a very young electorate in my constituency. While these are encouraging signs, we still need to make up for our low fertility rate with immigrants who share our values and want to stay with us longer term, and a foreign workforce that can contribute to our economy.

We need a foreign workforce also because our population is becoming better educated. Due to our successful education system, more Singaporeans will be taking up professional, managerial, executive and technical (PMET) jobs. But who is going to help you and complement you in the work that you do? As Chun Sing was saying, if our younger Singaporeans cannot find that kind of work here and they have a good education, you might end up with your sons and your daughters going somewhere else to work, which is really not the desired outcome. We need foreigners to complement our workforce. I have passed the chairmanship of the productivity committee on to [DPM Tharman Shanmugaratnam] at a very propitious time because we had just come out of the recession. Since productivity goes down during a recession and shoots up when you are coming out of the recession, I could declare victory and hand over to him. So he has the hard work of lifting productivity.

To improve productivity, we have put in place policies, such as encouraging companies with PIC grants, and to train and re-train workers. But it also requires really hard work on the ground to convince individuals to go for re-training. I think the unions have been doing a very good job. I am an advisor to the United Workers of Electronics & Electrical Industries (UWEEI), the electronics union, and they are having a very difficult time because electronics is one of the industries that faces the most rapid churn. Changes are taking place all the time. There are companies leaving and new companies entering the sector. Thus, a lot of training and re-training is required, which unions and employers work very closely together with the government agencies to facilitate.

Let me share one of the cases that I attended to in my Meet-the-People sessions about 10 years ago. This lady, who must have been in her late 30s, came to see me because her employer, SATS, had posted her to its newly completed second flight kitchen, SATS 2. She told me that she could not cope with the computerised equipment in the new kitchen, and found it too complicated to learn. I asked her, "How do you want me to help you?" She said, "Can you please help me to write a letter to the company to allow me to continue working where I was working before?" I tried to persuade her, reasoning that even if she worked in the old flight kitchen, the company could refurbish the old kitchen with new equipment in future. The training that her company was putting her through might, in fact, be good for her. She was persuaded by the argument but, at the end of it, all she said to me, "No, this is just too difficult. Can you please help me to write a letter to the company to request that I stay in my old job?"

Encouraging productivity requires hard work on the ground, to speak with and persuade individuals. Some of our union leaders have been quite outstanding at this task. I have spoken with some UWEEI union leaders who spend time talking to workers on the floor to persuade them to go for training courses. These workers have to work, sometimes overtime, and have families to look after. Our unions have been doing a lot of hard work, talking to people one by one.

Question: I am a medical doctor and a volunteer with a medical-related NGO. My question relates to the issue of intergenerational transfer of costs, particularly with regard to healthcare. The healthcare costs in Singapore are currently S$12–13 billion per year, of which the government funds about S$4 billion. Medisave, MediShield and Medifund make up about S$2 billion. In reality, for most of the people who are hospitalised and facing expensive hospital bills, their bills are actually paid by their children either out of pocket or through their Medisave. In order to be entitled to use Medifund, you have to exhaust your children's Medisave account first.

I think MediShield Life is a great improvement because the catastrophic illnesses and high-value illnesses will be taken care of. However, I am concerned that the next generation will still carry a significant burden with the deductible remaining at S$2,000 or S$3,000. Right now, we are in a situation where 50- or 60-year olds have five or six children so the burden is spread out among them. People in my generation, on the other hand, belong to the stop-at-two generation.

My question is whether the current system of MediShield Life for catastrophic illnesses and depending on the patient's children is sustainable, because it will place an extraordinary burden on the increasingly smaller families in Singapore in the future. Thank you.

DPM Teo: I think [the participant] has pointed to a very interesting phenomenon today. This is the reason why we introduced the Pioneer Generation Package and MediShield Life. Let me also elaborate on intergenerational transfers. Indeed, our pioneer generation grew up in a time when they had very little savings in their CPF and Medisave, and some of them did not even sign up for MediShield. They may subsequently have fallen ill, leading to pre-existing conditions that prevented them from being able to get full coverage for MediShield later on.

We were motivated to introduce the Pioneer Generation Package and MediShield Life because of such reasons. The Pioneer Generation Package is focused on healthcare. One can choose to have a S$10 cup of coffee or a S$1.50 cup of coffee. However, even with our best efforts at keeping healthy, being able to stay healthy and free from a need for medical care is not (fully) within our control. This is something that worries a lot of people in our pioneer generation, as well as their children. In coming out with these plans, we thought that we should focus on healthcare instead of spreading our resources to other areas so that our pioneer generation would be able to enjoy their golden and silver years with more reassurance. This is what we are doing for the Pioneer Generation Package in tandem with MediShield Life.

On the topic of intergenerational transfers, I think that quite a number of healthcare systems around the world design them in an irresponsible way — through an anonymous intergenerational transfer. This refers to the practice of taxing the next generation to fund the healthcare needs of the previous generation in an anonymous fashion and without any direct mutual obligation to each other. Transfers within the family, in contrast, are a more natural and organic way of doing it. In fact, this is not something to be discouraged because children may want to provide more than basic healthcare or basic housing for their parents. I think such an arrangement is not necessarily a bad thing, and is something to be encouraged within family groups. We should not remove that mutual responsibility within families through a more socialised system. This responsibility is a very personal issue and should not be anonymised as is done with a tax-and-spend system.

In the design of MediShield Life, we were indeed trying to avoid the intergenerational transfer. When MediShield was not compulsory, each age group had to pay the premium appropriate for the medical costs of that age group. This prevented people from waiting to enter MediShield until they were older to benefit from a cheaper rate (than would be appropriate for that age group). Because MediShield was not compulsory, we had to design it in this way to avoid people opting out when they were younger and opting in later at an advanced age.

MediShield Life is now compulsory. When you make it compulsory, you can perform the intergenerational transfer by yourself, for yourself. This works by contributing a higher proportion than required for your age group when you are young. This coincides with your greater earning capacity and surpluses, giving you the ability to pay higher premiums than needed at that age group. The slope is adjusted so that (compared to premiums today) you pay more when you are young and less when you are older. The intergenerational transfer now occurs within yourself, which makes the system fair. This intergenerational feature is a very important feature of the new MediShield Life. As we transition from MediShield to MediShield Life, the Pioneer Generation Package will be of great help to our pioneers and their children.

With regard to the issue of whether there should be an "excess" (an amount which the person insured has to pay before insurance cover kicks in), I think that the "excess" is a very important element. Health economists in many countries have found this to be an important feature of our healthcare system. There is a co-payment amount and a minimum amount, or an excess below which the individual is responsible for paying. This is quite an important feature to encourage responsible use of healthcare benefits. Without this, healthcare expenditure can be easily inflated, and it is not clear that a larger expenditure will greatly improve the effects on health.

This system is one of the reasons why we can maintain the premiums for MediShield and MediShield Life at a very affordable rate. Without this structure, if we allow for first-dollar claims, MediShield premiums and MediShield Life premiums will go through the roof. The system of excess is a crucial part of MediShield and MediShield Life, and many health economists find it a unique and important feature of our healthcare system.

During my efforts to explain MediShield Life and the Pioneer Generation Package, I spoke with 40 to 50 residents at a void deck a couple of months ago. One woman told me, "Our insurance system is terrible. My mother has to pay higher premiums as she grows older. She has to pay so much for her insurance". Her mother was around 73 years old. This woman continued to say, "My daughter is studying in the United States and it is wonderful there. The healthcare insurance system covers everything from the first dollar." So I asked her, "How much does your 73-year-old mother pay for her health insurance, and how much does your 23-year-old daughter pay for her health insurance?" It turned out that the annual premium paid by her mother was equal to what her daughter was paying in one month. That is indeed the impact of a health insurance system that is not designed to encourage responsible behaviour.

Question: My key takeaway from today's event is that Singapore, due to its very exceptional conditions and the context that we face, has had to make very pragmatic choices in the past and may have to do so in the future. This question is inspired by a conversation at my table about Mr Han Fook Kwang's column yesterday in *The Straits Times*. He wrote about three dark secrets that Singapore has had in order to achieve success today, including income inequality, growth at the expense of lowly-paid foreign workers and political suppression to some degree. In light of the 2011 general elections and the upcoming elections, how can we accommodate the new norm of political diversity without compromising our survival?

DPM Teo: Indeed, the choices that we had when we became independent 50 years ago were starker. They had to do with survival. Our choices were limited and you had to go with what you had. To use an analogy, it is a little bit like buying a Model T Ford. You could choose whichever colour you wanted, as long as it was black. By that means, Ford was able to provide motorcars. To stick with that example, Ford was able to provide mass transportation for many Americans but they had to accept that the Model T Ford was black. Today, you have a much more diverse range of interests and views, a luxury we did not have in the earlier years.

There are two important caveats there. The first is the assumption that we will continue to be in this happy situation where we do not encounter a major crisis, that we will have all the resources that we want and that we will have all the time in the world to have discussions before we decide. Second (caveat), the discussion and exchange of views is important. It remains a luxury which is important when we discuss these issues in an academic environment where we examine all possibilities. However, you can see that even in a small space like this with a variety of people, even though there is not a great diversity in backgrounds, it is not easy to come to an agreement on what exactly we should do. Some people will leave feeling dissatisfied. They will think that we should have done this or that, that we should have done a little bit more of this or a little bit more of that.

In the end, the karma of anyone who is in government, regardless of whether he runs the government or a town council, is such that he has to decide. He cannot carry on the conversation indefinitely. Otherwise, we might end up like London, which has been discussing the construction of a new airport for the last 30 to 40 years. It still has not been built and Heathrow Airport continues to become more crowded every year.

The situation [in Singapore] has indeed changed, and I would say for the better. More people have views, and these are useful views, which can be tapped on to improve the policymaking process and the choices that we have. In the end, however, it is the karma of the government that it has to decide to do this or that. You may not always be able to do everything that everybody wants. Following that, it will require a certain political maturity on the part of everyone in Singapore to say, "Yes, okay, we have had a good discussion. Let's go on, let's go ahead to move on, and we decide."

This is not unique to the political arena. Everyone faces it. If you are a teacher, your predecessors had an easier time because they were practically the only educated ones in society. Parents would send their children, probably sons (in those days) rather than daughters, to school and tell the teacher, "Can you please educate my child? I never had the benefit of education. If he is naughty, do give him a tight slap and tell me about it. When he comes home, I will give him a few more". That was how things were settled. Today, there are well-educated parents who will question you. "Why have you taught my son or my daughter in this way? Isn't this wrong? Haven't you told them the wrong thing? Should you be encouraging them to do something different?" You have to spend quite a lot of time, which is essential, on parent-teacher interactions in order to create an alignment between the parents, the home, the school and the child's upbringing. A lot of this happens today. It happens in school and in governance. Even our doctors are facing such issues. When a patient sees a doctor, it is not unusual for the patient to check the Internet to verify that the doctor is telling him the truth or he could be looking for multiple opinions while consulting the doctor.

Things have changed. I think they have changed for the better, but we also need a mature political process that allows us to end up with good solutions, to which we can say, "Okay, we accept it. Let's move on, and let's get it done as best we can," instead of looking at diversity as an objective in itself and ending up in gridlock, as a number of countries have done. For example, after elections in some European countries, they are unable to form a government for months, sometimes more than a year. I am not sure that we really want to end up in a situation like that. Chun Sing, do you have some comments on this?

Minister Chan: Let me answer the question in two segments. The first issue is about diversity and the second about fundamentals. Diversity in itself is not a weakness, diversity can be a strength. The key is not diversity per se, but how we as a society achieve convergence after sharing these diverse views. The world is becoming so uncertain that the more perspectives we have, the more we will be able to check our own blind spots as a society.

The question is whether we have the mechanism and maturity to find convergence beyond diversity and take our country forward. This is the most challenging part, and it takes a certain maturity to have a give-and-take relationship. It takes maturity to be more circumspect about having different views from someone else, to realise that it does not necessarily make us right and to think about why someone has taken a certain stand before shouting down his or her view. As Karl Marx would say, when there is a thesis, there is an anti-thesis. The challenge is to find that synthesis.

In order for us to find that synthesis, we have to put the greater good of our society and the future of our country ahead of our own preferences and desires. This is easy to say, but not always easy to do. Many people will passionately champion their own causes, and so they should. The question is, having championed our own causes, do we and are we able to embrace differences of opinion? Will we be able to find that synthesis and take the country forward? If we can do that, I think we will be much stronger.

On the issue of fundamentals, I have had conversations with many young people who are much younger than me. They tell me that we need a new narrative for our country, and I can understand and appreciate what they mean. We will find a new way to govern our society, which has gone beyond the basic tiers of Maslow's Hierarchy of Needs. We have gone up the hierarchy and gone beyond issues of security, safety, food and lodging. With a diverse population, we need to find a convergence of opinion. At the same time, I also share that we must not lose sight of the fundamentals. First, we need to make a living. If we cannot make a living and provide the opportunities for our younger generation and our people, I do not think that many people will treat our little red passport with much respect.

Our Prime Minister gets invited to the G20 conferences, not because we are one of the G20 countries. Many people have said that we have punched above our weight. Yes, we may have done that at this moment, but it is not a given that we will always and effortlessly be able to punch above our weight. I have never taken the idea that we will always be as successful as we are now, effortlessly, for granted. Fifty years ago, if we were to have named the three most successful South-east Asian countries that were seen as the rising stars, I think Singapore would not have been on the list. I think Ceylon, Burma and maybe the Philippines would have been on that list. The tide of history comes and goes, and we should never be complacent that just because we are where we are today, we will always be where we are tomorrow.

The second fundamental that befalls us is that we have to take care of our own security and independence. This goes back to the fact that we were never an independent country in this part of the world in the last 500 to 600 years. In World War II, someone asked the Australians and the New Zealanders why they were participating in the fight in Singapore when the Japanese were coming down the Malayan Peninsula. The blunt answer was that whatever happened in Singapore, if Singapore were to fall, they would be affected by it. Those are the fundamentals: making a living and taking care of our independence and security.

The third set of fundamentals is to always keep our society together. In the 1960s, our challenges with regard to keeping society together had to do with race, language and religion. It also had to do with the rich and the poor. Going forward, there will be new fault lines in our society. Some of them will be internal; others will be impacted by the larger forces around the world. We do not have our own indigenous language. We will be impacted and buffeted by the forces that are affecting the rest of the world. We cannot be free from that.

The question is, going forward, what are the new fault lines that will threaten to pull our society apart? How do we develop new structures and institutions to mitigate this? Take race and religion, for example. It took us many years to arrive at where we are today, where we have the interracial and religious confidence circle, the IRCCs. For us, when something happens, we are able to react rationally as Singaporeans first, not as Chinese, Indians or Malays. That took tremendous effort. Going forward, there will be new fault lines. The question is, will we be able to similarly put aside our individual agendas, come together and perhaps develop new mechanisms for us to manage these new fault lines?

If I may share one very poignant example over the last two years, I think the memories of the Little India riot are still fresh in many of our minds. It happened two Decembers ago, at the end of 2013. Many people will focus on the security situation in Little India during those critical hours, and on whether we were able to contain the riot and so forth. Indeed, it was a dicey situation in Little India at that point in time. I still remember what happened that night; I was covering the defence portfolio then. What went through my mind was not just what had happened in Little India that night, but whether it would spread. How would our Singaporean Indians react to this? How would our Chinese react to this? If we were to go back in history to 50 years ago and something like this had happened — a rumour had spread that a Chinese bus driver had knocked down an Indian and killed him — I am not so sure that the reaction would have been similar to what we saw during the Little India riot in 2013.

We may have reached a certain stage of maturity, but we can never be complacent because some things are very visceral. We never know when it will be sparked off again. This is just one example of some of the fundamentals that we are still grappling with, and we should never take them for granted.

Going forward, there will be other issues that might be as thorny as what race, language and religion used to be. We will have to find mechanisms to resolve some of these internal social tensions within our society. Yes, we will need a new narrative because we have gone beyond the basic needs of Maslow's Hierarchy of Needs. We now have more educated people, more diverse views and greater aspirations for self-actualisation. As we pursue all of this, let us also not forget some of the fundamentals within our society that will never go away: to be successful and relevant as a small nation in the face of global competition, to ensure that we will not be a footnote in history, to take care of our own sovereignty and security, to constantly find mechanisms to resolve the inherent tensions in our society on the social front and to pull everybody together and move forward as one united nation.

Question: I think this conversation has been fascinating because it demonstrates that Singapore is going through a major transition. It is also clear that many Singaporeans feel a sense of anxiety about the future. My question to both of you, if you had to help reduce this anxiety about the future among Singaporeans, what would you say to them?

Minister Chan: I would say two things. The anxiety that Singaporeans face, depending on our station in life, is not always the same. If I divide our population into three segments, the lowest-income segment will worry about whether their children will be able to catch up in the next generation. The middle-income group will worry about whether they will be able to catch up with the top one-third and if they will be able compete with the rest of the middle-income segment in the region and beyond. Even the top one-third will be anxious because, unlike in the past where the economic cycles were much longer and more predictable, they will be concerned about whether they will be able to entrench or retain their position in the top one-third.

My response to this is that I am confident that if we can pull together as a nation, there is no challenge that we cannot overcome. We started with much less and more existential challenges in 1965. The pioneer generation showed us what could be done by focusing their minds and energies. There is no reason why our generation, with much more, albeit also with much more complex challenges, cannot overcome such challenges. The crux of whether we can overcome obstacles is whether we can stay united as a people. The crux of whether we can stay united as a people is whether we can have a sense of shared perspective about our common challenges and put aside our individual preferences for the greater good, as well as constantly defend and enlarge the common space that we have as Singaporeans.

In order to do that, we have to stay rooted but constantly look for that forward-looking and inclusive identity. We have to look for a set of ideals that will guide us going into the future, to always move together as a nation, to always do more for those with less, to always remember our station in life as a small country, and not lose sight of some of these fundamentals. So I am confident, if we can do that.

DPM Teo: Indeed, the world has changed. The old certitudes do not hold anymore. If you take Japan as a model, for example, the idea of the salaryman and life-long employment in the same firm, job and line of work, perhaps even the same line of work that his father or grandfather did in the same firm, does not hold anymore. There are a number of reasons for this. First, we live and work a lot longer than we used to. Like I said, lifespans used to be shorter. More of us will have a work and life cycle that looks more like that of a football player or a ballerina. Let me explain what that means. The normal process, or what used to be considered normal, was to start work, get an increment every year, be promoted and keep getting more and more until you retire in a blaze of glory at the top of your job and your maximum salary. That has been a fairly typical model, especially if you use the example of the Japanese salaryman.

Today, we live longer and have different needs in our different life phases. We may be moving into a type of life cycle where we work very hard and have our maximum earnings at a certain age when our requirements are at their maximum. That may be when we have children, and the children have needs, when our parents have needs. Once your children are independent, you might choose to be economically active and work but in a different kind of job with a different kind of pace and pressure. This could be a part-time position. It is a little bit like a football player who has his peak earning years, then becomes a coach or manages a big football club after that. Or you could manage a school team or run a pub. At the same time, you save money and do not spend it unwisely, and that is your life cycle. Ballerinas are also like that. You cannot be in the top flight your entire life. And I think that the life cycles and the nature of work mean that each of us has to make this adaptation.

Teachers in schools are a good example. We have teachers who have retired as principals or heads of departments and returned to teach again. They come back as teachers and not principals or heads of departments. Somebody else will become the principal or head of department, but a wise principal will say, "Mr so-and-so, Mrs so-and-so or Madam so-and-so, you have a lot of experience. Can you take my weakest PSLE class and make sure that they pass mathematics this year?" That would be wonderful for her or him, for the pupils and for the system as a whole. He or she does not need to be principal or a head of department. It would require some adjustments to your pace of life or ego but I think many of us will go through this transition, and this is partly because of the kind of work we do. I think some of the anxiety is due to that.

The other source of anxiety, of course, is due to change. The nature of jobs is changing very rapidly. What you have learnt or trained in may become obsolete within your lifetime, maybe two or three times within your working lifetime. I studied computing when I was at university. We did not have laptop computers. The IBM PC had not even been invented when I started learning computer science. The amount of computing power in the machine in the computer science department was a lot less than what is in my handphone today. It is completely different. Technology has changed, and the life cycles of companies have changed too. The concept of lifetime employment is called into question when people live longer than companies. It used to be that companies lived longer than people across many generations, but now people live longer than their companies. You have heard all the stories about many companies that were in the Fortune 500 x years ago but are no longer there today. I think these are some of the anxieties that we are all facing.

There is also anxiety about values and how they are changing. The old certainties, certitudes and values seem to have changed. I had an old German friend, a general, who said that values were very clear in the old days. If a young man had a boy-girl problem, he consulted his elder brother or sister, his parents, his teachers or his uncles, and they would have given him approximately the same guidance about dealing with the issue. People held values that were more consistent and generally accepted and uniform in society. Now, if he were to ask all of these people, he might get the same answer from them but that answer would be for him to decide for himself. And so, what does he do? These are some of the anxieties that both young people and adults face in society today. The old certitudes are no longer there. How do we help people deal with these anxieties?

One of the solutions is a functional one: greater training and re-training opportunities. That is the mantra that we always put out, and it is real. When I was the Minister of Education, I had a choice to make. For a period of time, we had growing cohorts coming into the polytechnics, and we could see that. These were the cohorts between 1988 and 1997. We had to decide whether to allow more students into each of the four polytechnics or build a fifth polytechnic. We decided to build a fifth polytechnic because it would come in useful for continuing education and training for people in the future. We would need such institutions and facilities for the future. Continuing education and training is an important feature of dealing with some of these anxieties, and that has to become ingrained in us. If you look at the evolution of education in Singapore, we have gone from mass primary education to mass secondary education, and now mass tertiary education. The next step is mass continuing education. No country has achieved that today, and that is one evolution and innovation that we need to make. That is the functional part.

The other part is how to share the risk a little bit more, and this is indeed what we are working on with a number of things that we are doing. For example, MediShield Life is actually a form of risk pooling across the population. We are doing a number of these things in a sustainable and responsible way. Remember that a promise is worth something only if you can keep it. If you are writing a promise with a cheque underwritten by somebody else, it is not a promise at all. And so, there will be more risk pooling and helping each other to share the risk of the vicissitudes of life.

Third, we need to remain united and care for each other as a society, like a family. It is possible to do so because Singapore is small. We are not a huge country of two or three hundred million, or a billion people. We do not even have 50 or 60 million people. We are a small country — 3.5 million Singaporeans. Surely we can care for each other. We see examples of that every day. Our grassroots leaders and people in the VWOs [voluntary welfare organisations] are working selflessly for others and deriving their happiness and satisfaction, not from direct benefits but from seeing other people's happiness. I think we should strive to be more like these people.

These are some of the things we can do to deal with this anxiety. It is not simply what I say or what the government does, but also about what the individual does. The individual also has social responsibilities — to make sure that he remains employed, to ensure that he makes use of the safety nets in a responsible way and strive to contribute to the general happiness of society. We hope he derives more happiness and less anxiety from doing that too. I would say, to deal with the anxiety, let us go forward together. The road is easier, the load is lighter and we will have a jollier and happier time when we move forward together.

Janadas Devan: Thank you, Ministers. We have come to the end of another Singapore Perspectives. This year marks Singapore's 50th year of independence and this conference was pegged as part of the 50th anniversary commemorations. This conference has featured a variety of views on Singapore's past, present and future choices, but as DPM and Minister Chan indicated, there is a certain underlying confidence and agreement about the basics despite this diversity. Nobody after 50 years doubted that this should and shall be forever an independent and sovereign state. This is, in the context of our very young history of just 50 years, an amazing achievement.

Background Paper

CHAPTER 7

Study on the Perceptions of Singapore's History

LEONG CHAN-HOONG, MAGDALENE CHOO,
ELAINE HO, VARIAN LIM, PAVEENA SEAH
AND YANG WAI WAI

INTRODUCTION

The research objectives of the survey on public perceptions of local history are two-fold: (a) to identify critical historical events that resonate with Singaporeans and (b) to tease out different strains of narratives that predict present and future well-being among the different generations of Singaporeans. The creation and narration of the Singapore Story will be examined in relation to the theory of collective memory.

Collective memory is a shared representation of the past that is actively drawn on by groups of people for the purpose of finding their group identity (Griffin, 2004;[1] Liu & Hilton, 2005;[2] Olick, 1999;[3] Wertsch, 2008).[4] Discrete

---

[1] Griffin, L. J. (2004). "Generations and Collective Memory" Revisited: Race, Region, and Memory of Civil Rights. *American Sociological Review, 69*(4), 544–557.

[2] Liu, J. H., & Hilton, D. J. (2005). How the Past Weighs on the Present: Social Representations of History and their Role in Identity Politics. *The British Journal of Social Psychology, 44*(4), 1–21.

[3] Olick, J. K. (1999). Collective Memory: The Two Cultures. *Sociological Theory, 17*(3), 333–348.

[4] Wertsch, J. V. (2008). The Narrative Organization of Collective Memory. Ethos, *36*(1), 120–135.

episodes of events experienced by individuals are strung together into a coherent narrative through an active social negotiation process (Lee, Ramenzoni & Holme, 2010;[5] Olick, 1999;[6] Shahzad, 2012).[7] Collective memories are therefore both personal and shared.

At the individual level, the evaluation of historical events is often shaped by personal socio-demographic experience (Griffin, 2004;[8] Olick, 1999;[9] Schuman & Scott, 1989).[10] For example, in a study on the recollection of national or world events, participants were more likely to generate events that they had personally experienced in their formative years. Reasons such as "I was in the service" and "I lost friends" were commonly cited. Physical location and social identity also determine how well events are remembered. For example, Caucasians who lived near the epicentre of the American civil rights movement had better recall of the movement in the 1960s.

Similar to individuals' recall of events, memory of events among different groups of individuals is culture specific and influenced by the shared experience of people living in the same geographical space or nation-state (Liu et al., 2005, 2009, 2012).[11] Individuals in each nation-state, with shared

---

[5] Lee, S., Ramenzoni, V. C., & Holme, P. (2010). Emergence of Collective Memories. *PloS One, 5*(9), e12522.

[6] Olick, op. cit.

[7] Shahzad, F. (2012). Collective Memories: A Complex Construction. *Memory Studies, 5*(4), 378–391.

[8] Griffin, op. cit.

[9] Olick, op. cit.

[10] Schuman, H., & Scott, J. (1989). Generations and Collective Memories. *American Sociological Review, 54*(3), 359–381.

[11] Liu, J. H., Goldstein-Hawes, R., Hilton, D., Huang, L., Gastardo-Conaco, C., Dresler-Hawke, E., et al. (2005). Social Representations of Events and People in World History across 12 Cultures. *Journal of Cross-Cultural Psychology, 36*(2), 171–191. Liu, J. H., Paez, D., Slawuta, P., Cabecinhas, R., Techio, E., Kokdemir, D., ... Zlobina, A. (2009). Representing World History in the 21st century: The Impact of 9/11, the Iraq war, and the Nation-state on Dynamics of Collective Remembering. *Journal of Cross-Cultural Psychology, 40*(4), 667–92. Liu, J. H., Paez, D., Hanke, K., Rosa, A., Hilton, D. J., Sibley, C. G., ... Suwa, K. (2012). Cross-cultural Dimensions of Meaning in the Evaluation of Events in World History? Perceptions of Historical Calamities and Progress in Cross-cultural Data from Thirty Societies. *Journal of Cross-Cultural Psychology, 43*(2), 251.

representation of past events, collectively determine the country's norms and values, and consequently affect the strategies adopted when dealing with challenges (Liu & Hilton, 2005).[12]

In a cross-national study that assessed the opinion of 40 historical world events from 6,023 university students in 30 countries, Liu and associates identified three broad clusters of respondents based on their view of historical events (Liu et al., 2012).[13] Three groups of countries shared similar perspectives on history — a Western group and two non-Western groups. Countries in the same group broadly shared a similar historical fate as either an Anglo-Saxon colonial master or a secondary, regional outpost and/or colony.

The Western group comprised Australia, New Zealand, Europe[14] and the Americas. The first non-Western group of countries included China, Colombia, Japan, Mexico, Taiwan and Tunisia while the second group consisted of Canada, Fiji, Russia and Asia.[15] Generally, the countries' responses to events that exemplify historical calamities (e.g., World War II, September 11) were more similar than their responses to events that highlight historical progress (e.g., the first man on the moon and the invention of the printing press).

Events related to historical progress are mostly Western-based, and hence may not resonate with non-Western countries. Responses to historical calamities, on the other hand, affect people living in both Western and non-Western countries, and it predicted willingness to defend the country better than responses to historical progress. The findings further suggest that participants were more willing to fight to right the wrongs than to fight to achieve progress.

With this overarching view in mind, the present is anchored in the past and the past in the present: past events frame the interpretations of current events in order to develop a consistency and fidelity in communications and actions (Gongaware, 2010).[16] For instance, the focus on politics and war

---

[12] Liu & Hilton, op. cit.

[13] Liu et al., (2012), op. cit.

[14] Norway, Belgium, Italy, Switzerland, Austria, Germany, Netherlands, Hungary and Bulgaria.

[15] Hong Kong, India, the Philippines, Singapore, South Korea, Indonesia and Malaysia.

[16] Gongaware, T.B. (2010). Collective Memory Anchors: Collective Identity and Continuity in Social Movements. *Sociological Focus, 43*(3), 214.

summarises the roles and responsibilities of each stakeholder as well as highlights the positions of interdependency.

Communication through oral history or textbooks facilitates the transmission of these shared representations and their implications while physical symbols and symbolic rituals reinforce the message of the shared representations. Thus, the narrative that is weaved follows a generic schematic template where details of the events might vary but the overall theme stays constant (Wertsch, 2008).[17]

THE SINGAPORE NARRATIVE

Powerful national narratives are formed when diverse elements of the past are strung into a single, consistent, blemish-free shared representation of events (Hong & Huang, 2008).[18] The narrative serves to reinforce a sense of common destiny for the "ingroup" and emphasise the differences of the "outgroup" (Vasu, Chin & Law, 2014).[19] In its wake, a unique national identity is created and weaved into the consciousness of citizens (Hong & Huang, 2008).[20] The success of nation-building is thus contingent on the mass acceptance of the rhetoric (Ho, 2014).[21]

In Singapore, the National Education programme was introduced by the government in 1997 to promulgate the Singapore Story. The Singapore Story is one of overcoming the odds (Ghesquiere, 2011;[22] Tan, 2009).[23] It revolves

---

[17] Wertsch, op. cit.

[18] Hong, L., & Huang, J. (2008). *The Scripting of a National History: Singapore and its Pasts*. Hong Kong: Hong Kong University Press.

[19] Vasu, N., Chin, Y. & Law, K.Y. (2014). Un/Settled Narrations — Nationalism in the Asia Pacific. In N. Vasu, Y. Chin, & K. Y. Law (Eds.), *Nations, national narratives and communities in the Asia-Pacific* (pp. 1–8). New York, NY: Routledge.

[20] Hong & Huang, op. cit.

[21] Ho, S. H. (2014). Rethinking the Who, What and When: Why not Singaporean Military Heroes? In N. Vasu, Y. Chin, & K. Y. Law (Eds.), *Nations, national narratives and communities in the Asia-Pacific* (pp. 1–8). New York, NY: Routledge.

[22] Ghesquiere, H. (2011, June). From Third World to First: Singapore's Success. Paper presented at the ICAC 29th Caribbean Conference of Accountants, Kingston, Jamaica. Retrieved from http://www.nzcpr.com/wp-content/uploads/2013/12/Report-on-Singapores-Success-from-third-world-to-first.pdf

[23] Tan, S. (2009). Strategies of the PAP in the New Era. *East Asia Policy, 1*(4). Retrieved from http://www.eai.nus.edu.sg/Vol1No4_SamTan.pdf

around three critical periods: the Japanese Occupation, post-World War II and post-colonial/independent Singapore (Loh, 1998;[24] Hong & Huang, 2008).[25] These periods coincide with the themes of triumphing against external dangers posed by colonial masters and foreign occupiers, conquering domestic fault lines created by incompatible political ideologies, divisive ethnic-racial-religious politics and disparate language treatment as well as achieving economic prosperity in spite of the lack of natural resources (Ho, 2014;[26] Hong & Huang, 2008;[27] Loh, 1998).[28]

A thorough understanding of the Singapore Story is important in order to instil a sense of identity, belonging and unity (Lim, Yang, Leong & Hong, 2014;[29] Ong, 2010;[30] Vasu et al., 2014).[31] However, some have cautioned that the Singapore Story cannot end with Singapore being an economic miracle; nation-building is a work in progress and the perils of a small city-state can never be understated. Instead, this would be a good juncture to begin a dialogue and synthesis process to incorporate alternative and lay sides of the Singapore Story that are less economic in nature (Loh, 1998;[32] Ho, 2014;[33] Hong & Huang, 2008).[34]

The Singapore Story, which is currently "framed by the great person, the dramatic event and the distant period" (Ho, 2014, p. 22)[35] is becoming less relevant to the younger generation. As Singaporeans negotiate their position as

---

[24] Loh, K. S. (1998). Within the Singapore Story: The Use and Narrative of History in Singapore. Crossroads: *An Interdisciplinary Journal of Southeast Asian Studies, 12*(2), 1–21.

[25] Ho & Huang, op. cit.

[26] Ho, op. cit.

[27] Hong & Huang, op. cit.

[28] Loh, op. cit.

[29] Lim, S., Yang, W. W., Leong, C. H., & Hong, J. (2014). Reconfiguring the Singapore Identity Space: Beyond Racial Harmony and Survivalism, *International Journal of Intercultural Relations, 43*, 13–21.

[30] Ong, W.C. (2010). The Singapore Story: More than a State-Imposed Story. *RSIS Commentaries, 44*/2010.

[31] Vasu et al., op. cit.

[32] Loh, op. cit.

[33] Ho, op. cit.

[34] Hong & Huang, op. cit.

[35] Ho, op. cit.

citizens of the world, the one unified Singapore Story might be rendered obsolete, giving way to multiple strands of the story that speak to different segments of society (Kuah, 2012;[36] Lim et al., 2014).[37] It has been suggested that the success story should be augmented with the harmony and caring narrative (Mahbubani, 2014).[38] The harmony narrative relates to Singaporeans' ability to transcend racial identity and integrate the traditions of others into their way of life, and the caring narrative recounts the support that the less fortunate in society receives from the government.

In line with the research on collective memory of individuals and groups, different segments of Singapore's population may view historical events differently (Lim & Leong, 2016).[39] In a study that surveyed 460 Singaporean undergraduates, their perceptions of nation-building events (e.g., Changi Airport opens, Singapore joins ASEAN, the admission of Singapore into the UN), social resilience events (e.g., the bombing of McDonald House, the Bukit Ho Swee fire, Operation Cold Store) and reputational resilience events (e.g., the SARS outbreak, the Nicoll Highway collapse, Mas Selamat's escape) were evaluated. Respondents who indicated that nation-building events were important were associated with conservative political beliefs, more positive attitudes towards immigrants and a greater sense of rootedness. On the other hand, respondents who identified social resilience events as important have liberal political inclination.

In the present research, we will explore and examine critical historical events that form pillars of Singapore's present and future identity. Specifically, we wish to identify the parameters for customising the Singapore Story as well as the events and narratives that the Singapore Story should be built around. More importantly, we wish to examine how current and emerging narratives are correlated to how they view the future. After all, it is the shadow of history

---

[36] Kuah, A. W. J. (2012). Defining Singapore: Reconciling the National Narrative and the Global City Ethos. *RSIS Commentaries*, 196/2012.

[37] Lim et al., op. cit.

[38] Mahbubani, K. (2014, April 12). Three Stories to Strengthen the Singapore Spirit. *The Straits Times*. Retrieved from http://www.straitstimes.com/news/opinion/invitation/story/three-stories-strengthen-the-singapore-spirit-20140412

[39] Lim, S., & Leong, C. H. (2016). Casting the shadow of our past to illuminate the future of Singapore. *International Journal of Social Science and Humanity*, 6(5), 324–331.

that will inform the optimism for future well-being. Drawing from both theory and empirical findings, it is expected that people of different ages and races will have different perceptions of history.

The hypotheses of the study include:

1. Recent historical and highly impactful events are more likely to be remembered

2. Recollection of historical events are associated with the participants' age and ethnicity; older respondents recall more events than younger Singaporeans and events with a racial undertone are more likely to be recalled by the affected racial community

3. Historical narratives are to be explored using Exploratory Factor Analysis for the dimension measuring perceived importance of events. The relation between the derived narratives on current and expected well-being will be explored

4. In line with past empirical findings, historical events related to nation-building are likely to be rated as more important and favourable than events that highlight calamities

RESPONDENTS

A total of 1,516 Singaporean residents, consisting of Singaporean citizens aged 21 years and above were interviewed using a quota sampling method controlling for gender, age and race. The sample included 742 males and 774 females. The median age bracket was between 45 and 49 years. There were 1,148 Chinese (75.7%), 185 Malay (12.2%), 172 Indian (11.3%) and 11 others (0.7%).

INSTRUMENT

The questionnaire comprised demographic items, evaluations on 50 local historical events and measurements on personal well-being. The demographic items included age, gender, race, language spoken at home, housing type, employment status, occupation, monthly household income and highest education level attained.

For the evaluation of historical events, respondents were asked if they were aware of each of the 50 historical events in Singapore that occurred between

1819 and 2011. If they said they were aware of an event, they were then asked to express their agreement on a standardised five-point Likert scale for the following questions: perceived importance of the event to the respondent (1 = Not important, 5 = Very important); perceived importance to future generations of Singaporeans (1 = Not important, 5 = Very important); perception of event (1 = Negative event, 5 = Positive event); and their emotional reaction (1 = I don't feel anything at all, 5 = I feel strongly about it).

For the assessments on personal well-being, the respondents were asked to rate their perceived sense of satisfaction today, and five years into the future, using a Likert scale ranging from 1 (Very dissatisfied) to 5 (Very satisfied). Other than providing a broad indicator of well-being, the latter measuring expected satisfaction also reflects an overall sense of optimism for the future. Individuals who express a positive future outlook ostensibly hold a more optimistic view of their life.

PROCEDURE

Data was collected over a period of three months, from August 2014 to October 2014. The questionnaire was administered face-to-face, using the door-to-door method at randomly selected housing estates. Each interview took approximately 30 minutes to complete and was conducted by trained interviewers at the respondent's home. The survey was available in English, Chinese, Malay and Tamil.

Three rounds of pilot testing were conducted prior to administering the final questionnaire; two of them involved qualitative, face-to-face interviews with a total of 25 participants. The third was based on a quantitative survey involving more than 400 undergraduates from the Singapore Institute of Management (SIM).[40] The samples were representative and wide ranging, taking into consideration age, gender and ethnicity. On average, each pilot survey took 15 minutes.

In the first and second rounds of pilot testing, participants were asked about their awareness and perception of 53 key historical events in Singapore. In the third round of pilot testing, a questionnaire was administered to the undergraduates to check if the psychometric properties were reliable.

---

[40] Conducted by Dr Selina Lim, Associate Director of Teaching and Learning Centre, SIM University.

Participants were surveyed on their awareness and perception of 58 key historical events in Singapore, using a similar format to the final questionnaire.

Based on the three rounds of pilot testing, 50 key historical events were eventually selected. Given the limitations of the short interviewing time, the list of events had to be restricted to a reasonable number. Hence, only a sample of 50 historical events was selected.

SAMPLE CHARACTERISTICS

For the purpose of this report, the overall sample refers to all respondents surveyed in the study, that is, 1,516 participants. Table 1 shows the socio-demographic characteristics of the sample segmented by gender, age, ethnicity, citizenship, housing type and income. There were 742 and 774 male and female respondents, respectively. Respondents aged 50 and above comprised 37.7% of the sample, followed by respondents aged 35 to 49 (33.5%) and respondents aged 21 to 34 (28.8%).

Table 1 Socio-demographic characteristics of the sample

	Respondents	
	n	%
Gender		
Male	742	48.9
Female	774	51.1
Total	1,516	100.0
Age		
Age 21 to 34	437	28.8
Age 35 to 49	508	33.5
Age 50 and above	571	37.7
Total	1,516	100.0
Ethnicity		
Chinese	1,148	75.7
Malay	185	12.2
Indian	172	11.3
Others	11	0.7
Total	1,516	100.0

	Respondents	
	n	%
Citizenship		
At Birth	1,384	91.3
Naturalised	132	8.7
Total	1,516	100.0
Housing type		
HDB 1-, 2- & 3-room	294	19.4
HDB 4-room	677	44.7
HDB 5-room/Executive/HUDC	309	20.4
Executive Condo/Private Condo/Apartment/ Landed Property	236	15.6
Total	1,516	100.0
Household income per month		
S$2,999 and below	296	23.9
S$3,000–S$5,999	504	40.6
S$6,000 and above	440	35.5
*Total**	1,240	100.0
Education		
Non-tertiary educated	1,175	77.5
Tertiary educated	341	22.5
Total	1,516	100.0

*Note: Excludes respondents with "No Income", "Do not know" and "Refused"

Ethnic Chinese comprised 75.7% of the sample, followed by Malays (12.2%) and Indians (11.3%). The majority of respondents were Singaporean citizens at birth (91.3%) while a minority comprised naturalised Singaporean citizens (8.7%). The majority lived in four-room HDB flats (44.7%) while those living in five-room HDB, HDB executive and HUDC flats formed the second-largest group, with 20.4% of the sample. A large proportion (40.6%) of the sample fell within the monthly household income range of S$3,000 to S$5,999, and 35.5% of the respondents had a monthly household income of S$6,000 and above.

The following sections show the topline data on the six major assessments: (i) awareness of historical events, (ii) importance to respondent, (iii) importance to future generations, (iv) evaluation of events, (v) emotional intensity and (vi) life satisfaction.

AWARENESS

This section of the survey polled respondents' awareness of 50 key historical events. Table 2 shows awareness of all the events sorted in descending order.

Table 2   Ranked frequency of "awareness"

EVENTS	n	%
Opening of two Casinos (2010)	1500	98.9
SARS outbreak (2003)	1493	98.5
Major MRT breakdown (2011)	1461	96.4
Mas Selamat escapes (2008)	1443	95.2
Goh Chok Tong takes over as PM from Lee Kuan Yew (1990)	1411	93.1
WWII Japanese Occupation (1942)	1403	92.5
PAP loses Aljunied GRC (2011)	1392	91.8
Raffles' landing (1819)	1361	89.8
Lee Kuan Yew sobs on national TV over Separation (1965)	1344	88.7
Singapore hosts Youth Olympics (2010)	1327	87.5
Hotel New World collapse (1986)	1315	86.7
Completion of NEWater (2000)	1314	86.7
Introduction of GST (1994)	1291	85.2
NKF/TT Durai scandal (2005)	1255	82.8
Official launch of MRT (1988)	1244	82.1
Racial riots (1964)	1212	79.9
Singapore Cable Car accident (1983)	1185	78.2
Streaming in schools (1980)	1178	77.7
Launch of "Stop at Two" family planning (1970)	1144	75.5
Asian Financial Crisis (1997–98)	1142	75.3
Merger with Malaya (1963)	1108	73.1
Opening of Changi Airport (1981)	1101	72.6
Bukit Ho Swee fire (1961)	1072	70.7
Introduction of bilingualism policy in schools (1966)	1057	69.7
Formation of PAP (1954)	1038	68.5

EVENTS	n	%
Majulah Singapura is composed (1958)	1018	67.2
Jemaah Islamiyah terrorist plot (2002)	1012	66.8
Caning of Michael Fay (1994)	1010	66.6
Creation of Singapore national pledge (1966)	990	65.3
Singapore River clean-up campaign (1977)	970	64.0
First batch of NS men enlist (1967)	969	63.9
Formation of HDB (1960)	937	61.8
PAP wins GE (1959)	935	61.7
Hijack of SQ 117 (1991)	927	61.1
SQ 006 Taipei crash (2000)	907	59.8
Hock Lee bus riots (1955)	871	57.5
SilkAir flight crash in Palembang, Indonesia (1997)	863	56.9
Bombing of MacDonald House (1965)	798	52.6
Formation of SQ (1972)	770	50.8
Withdrawal of British troops (1971)	738	48.7
Introduction of Singapore currency (1967)	713	47.0
J.B. Jeyaretnam wins Anson by-election (1981)	669	44.1
Maria Hertogh riots (1950)	561	37.0
Formation of MAS (1970)	532	35.1
Merger of Nantah and University of Singapore (1980)	521	34.4
PAP splits (1961)	487	32.1
Debate on Graduate Mother Scheme (1984)	378	24.9
Laju hostage incident (1974)	335	22.1
"Marxist Conspiracy" plot uncovered, 16 people detained (1987)	281	18.5
Operation Cold Store (1963)	252	16.6

In line with hypothesis one, the top 10 events comprised the mostly recent, high impact or negative incidents such as the opening of the two casinos, the SARS outbreak, the major MRT breakdown, Mas Selamat's escape and the Japanese Occupation during World War II. At the other end of the spectrum, the events that respondents were least aware of are mainly security-related, including the Laju hostage incident, the "Marxist Conspiracy" and Operation Cold Store.

In line with hypothesis two, older as opposed to younger Singaporeans recalled more events (F (2, 1513) = 15.86, $p<0.001$). Respondents in the 21–34 year-old bracket recalled an average of 31.20 events (SD = 9.49), those in the 35–49 year-old group recalled an average of 33.02 events (SD = 10.12), and respondents aged 50 and above recalled an average of 34.72 events (SD = 9.91) (Table 3).

Table 3 Frequency of "awareness" by age groups (%)

EVENTS (in chronological order)	Total		Age 21-34		Age 35-49		Age 50 & Above	
	n	%	n	%	n	%	n	%
Raffles' landing (1819)	1361	89.8	409	93.6	451	88.8	501	87.7
WWII Japanese Occupation (1942)	1403	92.5	415	95.0	473	93.1	515	90.2
Maria Hertogh riots (1950)	561	37.0	181	41.4	157	30.9	223	39.1
Formation of PAP (1954)	1038	68.5	293	67.0	340	66.9	405	70.9
Hock Lee bus riots (1955)	871	57.5	243	55.6	242	47.6	386	67.6
Majulah Singapura is composed (1958)	1018	67.2	320	73.2	321	63.2	377	66.0
PAP wins GE (1959)	935	61.7	245	56.1	299	58.9	391	68.5
Formation of HDB (1960)	937	61.8	254	58.1	314	61.8	369	64.6
Bukit Ho Swee fire (1961)	1072	70.7	259	59.3	335	65.9	478	83.7
PAP splits (1961)	487	32.1	130	29.7	147	28.9	210	36.8
Operation Cold Store (1963)	252	16.6	57	13.0	75	14.8	120	21.0
Merger with Malaya (1963)	1108	73.1	323	73.9	361	71.1	424	74.3
Racial riots (1964)	1212	79.9	340	77.8	393	77.4	479	83.9
Bombing of MacDonald House (1965)	798	52.6	242	55.4	271	53.3	285	49.9
Lee Kuan Yew sobs on national TV over Separation (1965)	1344	88.7	380	87.0	451	88.8	513	89.8
Creation of Singapore national pledge (1966)	990	65.3	296	67.7	323	63.6	371	65.0
Introduction of bilingualism policy in schools (1966)	1057	69.7	276	63.2	355	69.9	426	74.6
Introduction of Singapore currency (1967)	713	47.0	180	41.2	222	43.7	311	54.5
First batch of NS men enlist (1967)	969	63.9	254	58.1	317	62.4	398	69.7

EVENTS (in chronological order)	Total		Age 21-34		Age 35-49		Age 50 & Above	
	n	%	n	%	n	%	n	%
Launch of "Stop at Two" family planning (1970)	1144	75.5	283	64.8	374	73.6	487	85.3
Formation of MAS (1970)	532	35.1	135	30.9	198	39.0	199	34.9
Withdrawal of British troops (1971)	738	48.7	199	45.5	239	47.0	300	52.5
Formation of SQ (1972)	770	50.8	197	45.1	274	53.9	299	52.4
Laju hostage incident (1974)	335	22.1	66	15.1	88	17.3	181	31.7
Singapore River clean-up campaign (1977)	970	64.0	255	58.4	318	62.6	397	69.5
Merger of Nantah and University of Singapore (1980)	521	34.4	109	24.9	168	33.1	244	42.7
Streaming in schools (1980)	1178	77.7	337	77.1	402	79.1	439	76.9
Opening of Changi Airport (1981)	1101	72.6	307	70.3	357	70.3	437	76.5
J.B. Jeyaretnam wins Anson by-election (1981)	669	44.1	126	28.8	202	39.8	341	59.7
Singapore Cable Car accident (1983)	1185	78.2	279	63.8	408	80.3	498	87.2
Debate on Graduate Mother Scheme (1984)	378	24.9	81	18.5	123	24.2	174	30.5
Hotel New World collapse (1986)	1315	86.7	322	73.7	455	89.6	538	94.2
"Marxist Conspiracy" plot uncovered, 16 people detained (1987)	281	18.5	68	15.6	92	18.1	121	21.2
Official launched of MRT (1988)	1244	82.1	326	74.6	420	82.7	498	87.2
Goh Chok Tong takes over as PM from Lee Kuan Yew (1990)	1411	93.1	387	88.6	478	94.1	546	95.6
Hijack of SQ 117 (1991)	927	61.1	258	59.0	331	65.2	338	59.2
Caning of Michael Fay (1994)	1010	66.6	244	55.8	364	71.7	402	70.4
Introduction of GST (1994)	1291	85.2	329	75.3	457	90.0	505	88.4
SilkAir flight crash in Palembang, Indonesia (1997)	863	56.9	180	41.2	317	62.4	366	64.1
Asian Financial Crisis (1997–98)	1142	75.3	311	71.2	406	79.9	425	74.4
Completion of NEWater (2000)	1314	86.7	388	88.8	438	86.2	488	85.5
SQ 006 Taipei crash (2000)	907	59.8	230	52.6	323	63.6	354	62.0

EVENTS (in chronological order)	Total		Age 21-34		Age 35-49		Age 50 & Above	
	n	%	n	%	n	%	n	%
Jemaah Islamiyah terrorist plot (2002)	1012	66.8	287	65.7	346	68.1	379	66.4
SARS outbreak (2003)	1493	98.5	432	98.9	502	98.8	559	97.9
NKF/TT Durai scandal (2005)	1255	82.8	347	79.4	431	84.8	477	83.5
Mas Selamat escapes (2008)	1443	95.2	429	98.2	481	94.7	533	93.3
Singapore hosts Youth Olympics (2010)	1327	87.5	392	89.7	460	90.6	475	83.2
Opening of two Casinos (2010)	1500	98.9	429	98.2	505	99.4	566	99.1
PAP loses Aljunied GRC (2011)	1392	91.8	382	87.4	477	93.9	533	93.3
Major MRT breakdown (2011)	1461	96.4	421	96.3	495	97.4	545	95.4

Historical events that have a racial undertone resonated more with the affected community. For instance, the Maria Hertogh riots (1950) and 1964 racial riots, Mas Selamat's escape (2008) and the Jemaah Islamiyah terrorist plot (2002) were more frequently recalled by the Malay respondents (Table 4) whilst the merger of Nantah (Nanyang University) and the University of Singapore (1980) was more often cited among the Chinese respondents. In essence, the results supported hypotheses one and two.

Table 4 Frequency of "awareness" by ethnic groups (%)

EVENTS (in chronological order)	Total		Chinese		Malay		Indian/Others	
	n	%	n	%	n	%	n	%
Raffles' landing (1819)	1361	89.8	1026	89.4	171	92.4	164	89.6
WWII Japanese Occupation (1942)	1403	92.5	1068	93.0	172	93.0	163	89.1
Maria Hertogh riots (1950)	561	37.0	378	32.9	103	55.7	80	43.7
Formation of PAP (1954)	1038	68.5	773	67.3	130	70.3	135	73.8
Hock Lee bus riots (1955)	871	57.5	656	57.1	119	64.3	96	52.5
Majulah Singapura is composed (1958)	1018	67.2	718	62.5	157	84.9	143	78.1
PAP wins GE (1959)	935	61.7	702	61.1	112	60.5	121	66.1

EVENTS (in chronological order)	Total		Chinese		Malay		Indian/Others	
	n	%	n	%	n	%	n	%
Formation of HDB (1960)	937	61.8	693	60.4	119	64.3	125	68.3
Bukit Ho Swee fire (1961)	1072	70.7	820	71.4	131	70.8	121	66.1
PAP splits (1961)	487	32.1	361	31.4	52	28.1	74	40.4
Operation Cold Store (1963)	252	16.6	190	16.6	34	18.4	28	15.3
Merger with Malaya (1963)	1108	73.1	844	73.5	130	70.3	134	73.2
Racial riots (1964)	1212	79.9	902	78.6	159	85.9	151	82.5
Bombing of MacDonald House (1965)	798	52.6	585	51.0	113	61.1	100	54.6
Lee Kuan Yew sobs on national TV over Separation (1965)	1344	88.7	1016	88.5	164	88.6	164	89.6
Creation of Singapore national pledge (1966)	990	65.3	724	63.1	133	71.9	133	72.7
Introduction of bilingualism policy in schools (1966)	1057	69.7	793	69.1	129	69.7	135	73.8
Introduction of Singapore currency (1967)	713	47.0	537	46.8	83	44.9	93	50.8
First batch of NS men enlist (1967)	969	63.9	723	63.0	129	69.7	117	63.9
Launch of "Stop at Two" family planning (1970)	1144	75.5	888	77.4	142	76.8	114	62.3
Formation of MAS (1970)	532	35.1	384	33.4	72	38.9	76	41.5
Withdrawal of British troops (1971)	738	48.7	564	49.1	82	44.3	92	50.3
Formation of SQ (1972)	770	50.8	559	48.7	94	50.8	117	63.9
Laju hostage incident (1974)	335	22.1	238	20.7	47	25.4	50	27.3
Singapore River clean-up campaign (1977)	970	64.0	745	64.9	113	61.1	112	61.2
Merger of Nantah and University of Singapore (1980)	521	34.4	421	36.7	43	23.2	57	31.1
Streaming in schools (1980)	1178	77.7	884	77.0	145	78.4	149	81.4
Opening of Changi Airport (1981)	1101	72.6	809	70.5	144	77.8	148	80.9
J.B. Jeyaretnam wins Anson by-election (1981)	669	44.1	474	41.3	97	52.4	98	53.6

	Total		Chinese		Malay		Indian/Others	
EVENTS (in chronological order)	n	%	n	%	n	%	n	%
Singapore Cable Car accident (1983)	1185	78.2	888	77.4	155	83.8	142	77.6
Debate on Graduate Mother Scheme (1984)	378	24.9	280	24.4	46	24.9	52	28.4
Hotel New World collapse (1986)	1315	86.7	1002	87.3	163	88.1	150	82.0
"Marxist Conspiracy" plot uncovered, 16 people detained (1987)	281	18.5	208	18.1	36	19.5	37	20.2
Official launch of MRT (1988)	1244	82.1	946	82.4	152	82.2	146	79.8
Goh Chok Tong takes over as PM from Lee Kuan Yew (1990)	1411	93.1	1073	93.5	163	88.1	175	95.6
Hijack of SQ 117 (1991)	927	61.1	692	60.3	113	61.1	122	66.7
Caning of Michael Fay (1994)	1010	66.6	776	67.6	126	68.1	108	59.0
Introduction of GST (1994)	1291	85.2	980	85.4	157	84.9	154	84.2
SilkAir flight crash in Palembang, Indonesia (1997)	863	56.9	637	55.5	124	67.0	102	55.7
Asian Financial Crisis (1997–98)	1142	75.3	887	77.3	128	69.2	127	69.4
Completion of NEWater (2000)	1314	86.7	983	85.6	169	91.4	162	88.5
SQ 006 Taipei crash (2000)	907	59.8	699	60.9	107	57.8	101	55.2
Jemaah Islamiyah terrorist plot (2002)	1012	66.8	745	64.9	150	81.1	117	63.9
SARS outbreak (2003)	1493	98.5	1131	98.5	182	98.4	180	98.4
NKF/TT Durai scandal (2005)	1255	82.8	971	84.6	140	75.7	144	78.7
Mas Selamat escapes (2008)	1443	95.2	1083	94.3	183	98.9	177	96.7
Singapore hosts Youth Olympics (2010)	1327	87.5	1012	88.2	151	81.6	164	89.6
Opening of two Casinos (2010)	1500	98.9	1140	99.3	179	96.8	181	98.9
PAP loses Aljunied GRC (2011)	1392	91.8	1057	92.1	163	88.1	172	94.0
Major MRT breakdown (2011)	1461	96.4	1098	95.6	182	98.4	181	98.9

IMPORTANCE TO RESPONDENTS

Respondents rated the importance of each event on a scale of 1 to 5 (1 = Not important to me at all, and 5 = Very important to me). Table 5 shows the mean scores of the scale sorted in descending order. On the whole, events linked to economic development and symbols of nationhood were seen as more important than political events. For instance, respondents attached more importance to the infrastructure-related developments, such as the opening of Changi Airport and the MRT, but not the "Marxist Conspiracy" or Operation Cold Store.

Table 5 Ranked mean score of "importance to respondent"

EVENTS	Mean (SD)
SARS outbreak (2003)	4.37 (0.76)
Official launch of MRT (1988)	4.36 (0.73)
Formation of HDB (1960)	4.23 (0.81)
Opening of Changi Airport (1981)	4.21 (0.80)
Creation of Singapore national pledge (1966)	4.20 (0.74)
Lee Kuan Yew sobs on national TV over Separation (1965)	4.14 (0.90)
Introduction of Singapore currency (1967)	4.14 (0.83)
Majulah Singapura is composed (1958)	4.11 (0.83)
Completion of NEWater (2000)	4.09 (0.82)
First batch of NS men enlist (1967)	4.07 (0.86)
Formation of PAP (1954)	4.07 (0.81)
Racial riots (1964)	4.04 (0.94)
Introduction of bilingualism policy in schools (1966)	4.04 (0.93)
Major MRT breakdown (2011)	4.02 (0.98)
PAP wins GE (1959)	4.01 (0.85)
Singapore River clean-up campaign (1977)	3.99 (0.89)
Introduction of GST (1994)	3.98 (0.91)
Jemaah Islamiyah terrorist plot (2002)	3.97 (0.94)
Asian Financial Crisis (1997–98)	3.91 (0.95)
Formation of MAS (1970)	3.90 (0.83)
Goh Chok Tong takes over as PM from Lee Kuan Yew (1990)	3.87 (0.93)
Mas Selamat escapes (2008)	3.86 (1.05)

EVENTS	Mean (SD)
WWII Japanese Occupation (1942)	3.84 (1.01)
Formation of SQ (1972)	3.84 (0.85)
Streaming in schools (1980)	3.78 (0.96)
Raffles' landing (1819)	3.69 (1.05)
Withdrawal of British troops (1971)	3.64 (1.02)
PAP loses Aljunied GRC (2011)	3.60 (1.01)
Singapore hosts Youth Olympics (2010)	3.58 (1.09)
Hotel New World collapse (1986)	3.58 (1.07)
NKF/TT Durai scandal (2005)	3.57 (1.13)
Merger with Malaya (1963)	3.55 (1.04)
Hijack of SQ 117 (1991)	3.54 (1.08)
Bombing of MacDonald House (1965)	3.48 (1.07)
PAP splits (1961)	3.46 (0.94)
Caning of Michael Fay (1994)	3.44 (1.16)
Maria Hertogh riots (1950)	3.40 (1.05)
Hock Lee bus riots (1955)	3.39 (1.05)
SQ 006 Taipei crash (2000)	3.39 (1.04)
SilkAir flight crash in Palembang, Indonesia (1997)	3.38 (1.05)
Merger of Nantah and University of Singapore (1980)	3.38 (1.00)
Laju hostage incident (1974)	3.36 (1.06)
Singapore Cable Car accident (1983)	3.35 (1.13)
Bukit Ho Swee fire (1961)	3.35 (1.09)
J.B. Jeyaretnam wins Anson by-election (1981)	3.32 (1.04)
"Marxist Conspiracy" plot uncovered, 16 people detained (1987)	3.29 (1.09)
Launch of "Stop at Two" family planning (1970)	3.28 (1.20)
Debate on Graduate Mother Scheme (1984)	3.27 (1.05)
Operation Cold Store (1963)	3.27 (1.04)
Opening of two Casinos (2010)	3.09 (1.27)

IMPORTANCE TO FUTURE GENERATIONS

This section of the survey asked respondents to gauge how important these events will be to future generations on a scale of 1 to 5, where 1 is "Not important to future generations at all" and 5 is "Very important to future generations". Table 6 shows the mean scores of "Importance to future generations", sorted in descending order. Respondents found the official launch of the MRT (M = 4.45, SD = 0.70) to be very important to future generations. Conversely, the "Stop at Two" family planning programme (M = 3.36, SD = 1.21) was not deemed important to future generations at all. In general, respondents found the creation of national symbols, such as the national pledge, to be highly important to future generations.

Table 6 Ranked mean score of "importance to future generations"

EVENTS	Mean (SD)	EVENTS	Mean (SD)
Official launch of MRT (1988)	4.45 (0.70)	Asian Financial Crisis (1997–98)	3.99 (0.91)
SARS outbreak (2003)	4.42 (0.74)	Streaming in schools (1980)	3.98 (0.93)
Introduction of bilingualism policy in schools (1966)	4.34 (0.78)	Caning of Michael Fay (1994)	3.85 (1.07)
Creation of Singapore national pledge (1966)	4.32 (0.68)	Withdrawal of British troops (1971)	3.83 (0.99)
Opening of Changi Airport (1981)	4.32 (0.78)	NKF/TT Durai scandal (2005)	3.82 (1.05)
Formation of HDB (1960)	4.31 (0.77)	Hijack of SQ 117 (1991)	3.81 (0.98)
First batch of NS men enlist (1967)	4.28 (0.78)	PAP loses Aljunied GRC (2011)	3.80 (0.96)
Completion of NEWater (2000)	4.28 (0.76)	Maria Hertogh riots (1950)	3.79 (1.05)
Racial riots (1964)	4.26 (0.88)	Hotel New World collapse (1986)	3.78 (1.03)
Majulah Singapura is composed (1958)	4.25 (0.74)	Merger with Malaya (1963)	3.74 (1.04)
Lee Kuan Yew sobs on national TV over Separation (1965)	4.24 (0.87)	Bombing of MacDonald House (1965)	3.73 (0.99)
Introduction of Singapore currency (1967)	4.22 (0.79)	Hock Lee bus riots (1955)	3.67 (1.06)
Jemaah Islamiyah terrorist plot (2002)	4.22 (0.83)	Laju hostage incident (1974)	3.65 (1.00)

EVENTS	Mean (SD)	EVENTS	Mean (SD)
Formation of PAP (1954)	4.18 (0.80)	PAP splits (1961)	3.61 (1.00)
Major MRT breakdown (2011)	4.16 (0.90)	Merger of Nantah and University of Singapore (1980)	3.59 (0.99)
Singapore River clean-up campaign (1977)	4.12 (0.87)	"Marxist Conspiracy" plot uncovered, 16 people detained (1987)	3.59 (1.05)
PAP wins GE (1959)	4.11 (0.82)	SilkAir flight crash in Palembang, Indonesia (1997)	3.56 (1.05)
WWII Japanese Occupation (1942)	4.10 (0.99)	Operation Cold Store (1963)	3.56 (1.07)
Mas Selamat escapes (2008)	4.05 (0.95)	Bukit Ho Swee fire (1961)	3.56 (1.10)
Formation of MAS (1970)	4.05 (0.78)	SQ 006 Taipei crash (2000)	3.56 (1.03)
Introduction of GST (1994)	4.02 (0.90)	Singapore Cable Car accident (1983)	3.55 (1.08)
Raffles' landing (1819)	4.01 (0.99)	Debate on Graduate Mother Scheme (1984)	3.47 (1.02)
Formation of SQ (1972)	4.01 (0.78)	J.B. Jeyaretnam wins Anson by-election (1981)	3.45 (1.01)
Singapore hosts Youth Olympics (2010)	3.99 (0.98)	Opening of two Casinos (2010)	3.43 (1.23)
Goh Chok Tong takes over as PM from Lee Kuan Yew (1990)	3.99 (0.89)	Launch of "Stop at Two" family planning (1970)	3.36 (1.21)

EVALUATION OF EVENTS AS NEGATIVE OR POSITIVE

This section of the survey asked respondents to describe the events as negative or positive on a scale of 1 to 5, where 1 is "Negative event" and 5 is "Positive event". Table 7 shows the mean scores of "Negative or positive events", sorted in descending order. Respondents deemed the MRT's official launch as the most positive event (M = 4.52, SD = 0.70) while the crash of the SilkAir flight in Palembang, Indonesia, was deemed the most negative event (M = 1.70, SD = 1.05). In general, progressive national development events, such as the Singapore River clean-up campaign, were considered positive events.

173

Conversely, civil disasters such as the collapse of Hotel New World were considered negative events.

Table 7 Ranked mean score of "negative or positive events"

EVENTS	Mean (SD)	EVENTS	Mean (SD)
Official launch of MRT (1988)	4.52 (0.70)	PAP splits (1961)	3.05 (1.02)
Opening of Changi Airport (1981)	4.43 (0.74)	Debate on Graduate Mother Scheme (1984)	2.96 (1.12)
Singapore River clean-up campaign (1977)	4.33 (0.76)	Operation Cold Store (1963)	2.84 (1.15)
Creation of Singapore national pledge (1966)	4.33 (0.73)	Launch of "Stop at Two" family planning (1970)	2.78 (1.14)
Introduction of Singapore currency (1967)	4.31 (0.74)	Opening of two Casinos (2010)	2.71 (1.20)
Majulah Singapura is composed (1958)	4.28 (0.80)	"Marxist Conspiracy" plot uncovered, 16 people detained (1987)	2.70 (1.18)
Formation of HDB (1960)	4.27 (0.84)	Introduction of GST (1994	2.53 (1.16)
Completion of NEWater (2000)	4.22 (0.91)	Laju hostage incident (1974)	2.19 (1.25)
Formation of SQ (1972)	4.19 (0.76)	Maria Hertogh riots (1950)	2.15 (1.19)
Introduction of bilingualism policy in schools (1966)	4.18 (0.91)	Hock Lee bus riots (1955)	2.13 (1.16)
Raffles' landing (1819)	4.17 (0.86)	WWII Japanese Occupation (1942)	2.05 (1.30)
First batch of NS men enlist (1967)	4.13 (0.91)	Bukit Ho Swee fire (1961)	1.97 (1.17)
Singapore hosts Youth Olympics (2010)	4.09 (0.90)	Racial riots (1964)	1.96 (1.27)
Formation of MAS (1970)	4.08 (0.84)	Asian Financial Crisis (1997–98)	1.95 (1.14)
Formation of PAP (1954)	4.07 (0.88)	Hijack of SQ 117 (1991)	1.93 (1.14)
PAP wins GE (1959)	4.07 (0.84)	Singapore Cable Car accident (1983)	1.91 (1.18)

EVENTS	Mean (SD)	EVENTS	Mean (SD)
Lee Kuan Yew sobs on national TV over Separation (1965)	4.01 (1.06)	Major MRT breakdown (2011)	1.88 (1.20)
Goh Chok Tong takes over as PM from Lee Kuan Yew (1990)	3.96 (0.86)	Bombing of MacDonald House (1965)	1.86 (1.12)
Withdrawal of British troops (1971)	3.73 (0.96)	Mas Selamat escapes (2008)	1.86 (1.17)
Merger of Nantah and University of Singapore (1980)	3.57 (0.96)	NKF/TT Durai scandal (2005)	1.81 (1.10)
J.B. Jeyaretnam wins Anson by-election (1981)	3.43 (0.98)	SQ 006 Taipei crash (2000)	1.80 (1.06)
Caning of Michael Fay (1994)	3.40 (1.31)	SARS outbreak (2003)	1.78 (1.25)
Streaming in schools (1980)	3.35 (1.13)	Hotel New World collapse (1986)	1.77 (1.15)
PAP loses Aljunied GRC (2011)	3.26 (1.07)	Jemaah Islamiyah terrorist plot (2002)	1.77 (1.18)
Merger with Malaya (1963)	3.11 (1.06)	SilkAir flight crash in Palembang, Indonesia (1997)	1.70 (1.05)

EMOTIONAL INTENSITY

This section of the survey asked respondents to rate how they feel emotionally about the events on a scale of 1 to 5, where 1 represents "I do not feel anything at all" and 5 represents "I feel very strongly about this". Table 8 shows the mean scores of emotional intensity, sorted in descending order. Respondents found the SARS outbreak (M = 4.17, SD = 0.89) to be highly emotional while most were indifferent towards Operation Cold Store (M = 3.04, SD = 1.00). In general, respondents felt strongly about national development events, such as the announcement of the separation from Malaysia when Lee Kuan Yew sobbed on national television. In contrast, respondents felt less strongly about the splitting of the People's Action Party in 1961.

Table 8 Ranked mean score of "emotional intensity"

EVENTS	Mean (SD)	EVENTS	Mean (SD)
SARS outbreak (2003)	4.17 (0.89)	WWII Japanese Occupation (1942)	3.54 (1.09)
Official launch of MRT (1988)	4.14 (0.90)	Singapore hosts Youth Olympics (2010)	3.52 (1.07)
Opening of Changi Airport (1981)	4.00 (0.91)	NKF/TT Durai scandal (2005)	3.51 (1.15)
Creation of Singapore national pledge (1966)	3.95 (0.94)	SilkAir flight crash in Palembang, Indonesia (1997)	3.47 (1.02)
First batch of NS men enlist (1967)	3.89 (0.96)	PAP loses Aljunied GRC (2011)	3.43 (1.02)
Majulah Singapura is composed (1958)	3.89 (1.00)	Caning of Michael Fay (1994)	3.40 (1.12)
Introduction of bilingualism policy in schools (1966)	3.88 (0.99)	Hijack of SQ 117 (1991)	3.38 (1.04)
Major MRT breakdown (2011)	3.87 (0.99)	SQ 006 Taipei crash (2000)	3.38 (0.99)
Formation of HDB (1960)	3.86 (0.99)	Withdrawal of British troops (1971)	3.36 (1.09)
Lee Kuan Yew sobs on national TV over Separation (1965)	3.85 (1.03)	Bombing of MacDonald House (1965)	3.33 (1.51)
Introduction of Singapore currency (1967)	3.85 (0.96)	Opening of two Casinos (2010)	3.26 (1.14)
Completion of NEWater (2000)	3.84 (0.98)	Singapore Cable Car accident (1983)	3.25 (1.05)
Racial riots (1964)	3.76 (1.01)	Merger of Nantah and University of Singapore (1980)	3.23 (1.02)
Jemaah Islamiyah terrorist plot (2002)	3.75 (1.01)	Debate on Graduate Mother Scheme (1984)	3.21 (0.97)
Singapore River clean-up campaign (1977)	3.74 (1.07)	Launch of "Stop at Two" family planning (1970)	3.20 (1.11)
PAP wins GE (1959)	3.73 (0.96)	Bukit Ho Swee fire (1961)	3.19 (1.09)
Introduction of GST (1994)	3.70 (0.94)	Raffles' landing (1819)	3.17 (1.13)
Formation of PAP (1954)	3.66 (0.99)	Maria Hertogh riots (1950)	3.15 (1.07)

EVENTS	Mean (SD)	EVENTS	Mean (SD)
Mas Selamat escapes (2008)	3.65 (1.09)	J.B. Jeyaretnam wins Anson by-election (1981)	3.14 (1.05)
Asian Financial Crisis (1997–98)	3.65 (1.02)	Merger with Malaya (1963)	3.13 (1.04)
Formation of SQ (1972)	3.63 (1.00)	Laju hostage incident (1974)	3.12 (1.10)
Formation of MAS (1970)	3.61 (1.02)	Hock Lee bus riots (1955)	3.11 (1.05)
Streaming in schools (1980)	3.58 (0.95)	PAP splits (1961)	3.09 (0.95)
Goh Chok Tong takes over as PM from Lee Kuan Yew (1990)	3.56 (1.01)	"Marxist Conspiracy" plot uncovered, 16 people detained (1987)	3.09 (1.13)
Hotel New World collapse (1986)	3.56 (1.06)	Operation Cold Store (1963)	3.04 (1.00)

LIFE SATISFACTION

This section of the survey polled respondents' life satisfaction five years ago, at present and five years from now, using a scale of 1 to 5, where 1 is "Very dissatisfied" and 5 is "Very satisfied". Tables 9 to 12 show respondents' present and future life satisfaction ratings, by age and ethnicity. In general, a majority (51.2%) of the respondents were satisfied with their lives five years ago. Similarly, a majority of the respondents (52.3%) were satisfied with their lives today. However, comparatively fewer (40.6%) respondents thought that they would be satisfied with their lives five years from now.

Table 9 Respondents' present life satisfaction by age groups (%)

Life satisfaction rating (at present)	Total		Age 21 to 34		Age 35 to 49		Age 50 and above	
	n	%	n	%	n	%	n	%
Very Dissatisfied	22	1.5	10	2.3	3	0.6	9	1.6
Dissatisfied	165	10.9	41	9.4	53	10.4	71	12.4
Neutral	442	29.2	121	27.7	162	31.9	159	27.8
Satisfied	793	52.3	237	54.2	258	50.8	298	52.2
Very Satisfied	94	6.2	28	6.4	32	6.3	34	6.0
Total	1516	100.0	437	100.0	508	100.0	571	100.0

Table 10 Respondents' future life satisfaction by age groups (%)

Life satisfaction rating (5 years from now)	Total		Age 21 to 34		Age 35 to 49		Age 50 and above	
	n	%	n	%	n	%	n	%
Very Dissatisfied	33	2.2	6	1.4	14	2.8	13	2.3
Dissatisfied	161	10.6	39	8.9	53	10.4	69	12.1
Neutral	569	37.5	150	34.3	187	36.8	232	40.6
Satisfied	616	40.6	183	41.9	212	41.7	221	38.7
Very Satisfied	137	9.0	59	13.5	42	8.3	36	6.3
Total	1516	100.0	437	100.0	508	100.0	571	100.0

Table 11 Mean score of life satisfaction by age groups

Life satisfaction rating	Total	Age 21 to 34	Age 35 to 49	Age 50 and above
	Mean (SD)	Mean (SD)	Mean (SD)	Mean (SD)
How satisfied are you with your life today?	3.51 (0.82)	3.53 (0.84)	3.52 (0.79)	3.49 (0.84)
How satisfied do you think you would be with your life five years from now?	3.44 (0.88)	3.57 (0.88)	3.42 (0.89)	3.35 (0.86)

Table 12 Mean score of life satisfaction by ethnic groups

Life Satisfaction Rating	Total	Chinese	Malay	Indian/ Others
	Mean (SD)	Mean (SD)	Mean (SD)	Mean (SD)
How satisfied are you with your life today?	3.51 (0.82)	3.47 (0.83)	3.59 (0.80)	3.64 (0.80)
How satisfied do you think you would be with your life five years from now?	3.44 (0.88)	3.40 (0.87)	3.54 (0.85)	3.57 (0.91)

UNCOVERING HISTORICAL NARRATIVES

In order to distil the social representation of historical events and how they are narrated, we subjected the data measuring "Importance to Respondents" to an exploratory factor analysis. We first selected the top 35 events based on the degree of event awareness, i.e., the top 35 events known to at least 60% of the respondents.[41] The events were organised around three latent factors or themes, each offering a unique lens to the type of events or lessons learnt. The three factors explained a total of 32.2% of the data variance, with nation-building contributing 21.2%, differences contributing 6.7% and national resilience contributing 4.3%, respectively. To aid in the interpretation of these three factors or themes, further analyses were performed.[42] Results (Table 13) showed the three components and the type of events associated with the factor. All events loaded primarily on one factor.

Table 13 Pattern matrix for importance to respondent using PAF with Promax rotation of three factor solution

Events	Nation Building	Differences	National Resilience
Majulah Singapura is composed (1958)	0.658	-0.190	0.081
Formation of HDB (1960)	0.646	0.076	-0.228
Creation of Singapore national pledge (1966)	0.586	-0.085	0.043
Formation of PAP (1954)	0.581	-0.065	-0.013
PAP wins GE (1959)	0.556	0.078	-0.081
Opening of Changi Airport (1981)	0.545	-0.133	0.083
Official launch of MRT (1988)	0.517	0.001	-0.028
First batch of NS men enlist (1967)	0.389	0.031	0.053
Lee Kuan Yew sobs on national TV over Separation (1965)	0.372	0.259	-0.055
Singapore River clean-up campaign (1977)	0.364	-0.045	0.223
Goh Chok Tong takes over as PM from Lee Kuan Yew (1990)	0.326	0.195	0.109
Completion of NEWater (2000)	0.303	0.214	0.013
Raffles' landing	0.290	-0.005	0.110
Opening of two Casinos (2010)	-0.288	0.515	-0.030
Asian Financial Crisis (1997–98)	-0.083	0.509	0.047

---

[41] The rating scores for the scale of these events were factor analysed. Bartlett's Test of Sphericity was significant (p<0.001) and the Kaiser-Meyer-Olkin measure of sampling adequacy value of 0.92 supported the factorability of the matrix. Principal Axis Factoring (PAF) suggests three factors with eigenvalues exceeding 1.

[42] Using Promax rotation, with factor loadings of at least 0.30.

Events	Nation Building	Differences	National Resilience
PAP loses Aljunied GRC (2011)	-0.023	**0.508**	0.012
Introduction of GST (1994)	0.064	**0.503**	-0.148
Merger with Malaya (1963)	-0.040	**0.472**	0.059
Major MRT breakdown (2011)	0.012	**0.422**	0.064
Streaming in schools (1980)	0.076	**0.414**	-0.110
Mas Selamat escapes (2008)	-0.003	**0.389**	0.270
Launch of "Stop at Two" family planning (1970)	-0.087	**0.381**	0.137
SARS outbreak (2003)	0.175	**0.358**	0.041
Racial riots (1964)	0.149	**0.329**	0.113
Introduction of bilingualism policy in schools (1966)	0.185	**0.306**	-0.015
Jemaah Islamiyah terrorist plot (2002)	0.100	0.273	0.151
WWII Japanese Occupation (1942)	0.034	0.259	0.063
NKF/TT Durai scandal (2005)	0.063	0.259	0.247
Hotel New World collapse (1986)	0.018	-0.147	**0.787**
Singapore Cable Car accident (1983)	-0.035	-0.054	**0.769**
SQ 006 Taipei crash (2000)	-0.044	0.040	**0.536**
Hijack of SQ 117 (1991)	-0.045	0.178	**0.452**
Bukit Ho Swee fire (1961)	0.061	0.035	**0.373**
Caning of Michael Fay (1994)	-0.004	0.247	**0.334**
Singapore hosts Youth Olympics (2010)	0.120	0.144	**0.300**

The nation-building dimension highlights the progress and achievements of Singapore over the years, including the building and enhancement of physical infrastructure and amenities such as the MRT and Changi Airport, as well as the creation of national symbols like the pledge and Singapore's separation from Malaysia. The differences dimension reflects historical choices that echo contestations, dilemmas and polarising views, for instance, the unravelling of the Jemaah Islamiyah terrorist plot, the "Stop at Two" birth control policy, the bilingualism policy and racial riots. Lastly, the dimension measuring national resilience highlights the tenacious and tumultuous challenges that Singaporeans have overcome since independence, including the cable car accident in the 1980s and the Bukit Ho Swee fire in the 1960s.

To explore the impact of age on the three sets of narratives, respondents were first divided into three age groups (21 to 34 years; 35 to 49 years; 50 years and above), followed by a one-way between-groups analysis of variance (ANOVA) on each of the three narratives. The one-way between-groups ANOVA showed a statistically significant difference in the nation-building component for all three age groups: F (2, 1513) = 17.82, p<0.001, η^2 = 0.02 (Table 14). Post-hoc comparisons using the LSD test indicated that the mean score of all three age groups were significantly different. Table 3 also shows a statistically significant difference in the national resilience component between the three age groups: F (2, 1513) = 8.04, p<0.001, η^2 = 0.01. Post-hoc comparisons using the LSD test indicated that the mean score of those aged 50 and above (M = 0.12, SD = 1.01) was significantly higher than those aged 21 to 34 (M = -0.08, SD = 0.77) and those aged 34 to 49 (M = -0.07, SD = 0.89).

CORRELATIONS BETWEEN HISTORICAL NARRATIVES AND LIFE SATISFACTION

Exploratory factor analyses identified three latent factors for the scale measuring importance to respondent. These were nation-building, differences and national resilience. Bivariate correlations between the three factors and past and present life satisfaction were examined.

Table 14 shows significant positive correlations between all three factors and present life satisfaction. The increased rating on historical events linked to nation-building, differences and national resilience is associated with higher levels of current satisfaction (r = 0.12, p<0.001; r=0.06, p<0.05; r=0.09, p<0.001, respectively).

Table 14 Impact of age on the three factors of importance to respondent

Importance to respondent	Mean (SD)			F	eta Sq
	Age 21 to 34	Age 35 to 49	Age 50 and above		
Nation Building	-0.17 (0.88)ₐ	-0.05 (0.90)ᵦ	0.17 (0.93)𝒸	17.82***	0.02
Differences	-0.04 (0.78)ₐ	-0.02 (0.94)ₐ	0.05 (0.96)ₐ	1.46	0.00
National Resilience	-0.08 (0.77)ₐ	-0.07 (0.89)ₐ	0.12 (1.01)ᵦ	8.04***	0.01

Note: *p<0.05, **p<0.01, ***p<0.001. Means with differing subscripts within rows are significantly different at the p<0.05 based on the LSD post-hoc test.

The two dimensions measuring nation-building and differences are not significantly correlated with perceived future life satisfaction (Table 15). However, national resilience is marginally correlated with perceived future life satisfaction. In other words, respondents who rated highly on the significance of historical events linked to national resilience (e.g., the collapse of Hotel New World) were more likely to feel optimistic about their future well-being.

Table 15 Correlations between the factors of importance to respondent and life satisfaction

Factors of Importance to respondent	Pearson's Correlations Coefficients	
	Present Life Satisfaction (N = 1,516)	Future Life Satisfaction (N = 1,516)
Nation Building	0.12***	-0.02
Differences	0.06*	0.02
National Resilience	0.09***	0.05+

Note: +p=0.06, *p<0.05, **p<0.01, ***p<0.001.

DISCUSSION

The study aims to find out how Singaporeans feel about major local historical events and uncover the underlying narratives in our history and its relationship with current and future satisfaction. As expected, recent events were more likely to be recognised by respondents. In line with findings in the literature on collective memories, the results show that people of different ages and races perceived historical events differently. Specifically, older Singaporeans recalled more events than the younger generations, and events with a racial undertone were more likely to be recalled by the affected ethnic community.

It was interesting that some events which were not experienced by the respondents maintained a high level of recognition (e.g., Raffles' landing, the Japanese Occupation during World War II, Lee Kuan Yew sobbing on national TV after separation from Malaysia) while some events which were likely to have been experienced registered lower levels of recognition (e.g., the Graduate Mothers' Scheme, the "Marxist Conspiracy" plot). Historical events that are widely recognised are anchors of nationhood; these events are also covered extensively in the media and in the national education curriculum.

The level of awareness was not always congruent with perceived importance of events: some events that were widely known were not perceived as important. For example, most people were aware of the opening of the two casinos (98%) but it obtained the lowest mean score in terms of importance (3.09). On the whole, respondents often felt that events that were important to them were also important for future generations of Singaporeans. Most historical events were rated differently depending on the measurements used. Responses to perceived importance, evaluation (i.e., positive or negative) and emotional connection were scored differently for each historical episode.

Further analysis on perceived importance identified three latent factors or narratives: nation-building, differences and national resilience. Nation-building events underscore the progress and development that Singapore has achieved over the years. These include the country's built-up physical infrastructure, like the MRT and Changi Airport, and symbols of nationhood such as the creation of the national pledge and Singapore's separation from Malaysia. Historical events that embody differences emphasise contestations, disagreements and dilemmas that contrast polarising opinions or perspectives, such as the Asian Financial Crisis and the foiling of the Jemaah Islamiyah terrorist plot as well as the "Stop at Two" birth control policy, the bilingualism policy and racial riots. Finally, events related to national resilience highlight the challenges and tribulations that Singaporeans have overcome as a people. Examples include the cable car accident in the 1980s and the Bukit Ho Swee fire in the 1960s.

In line with the theoretical and empirical observations in collective memory research, the current data suggest that events associated with economic development and symbols of nationhood are seen as more important than political and doctrinal events; events loaded on nation-building are also rated highly on the importance dimension. All three dimensions — nation-building, differences and national resilience — are positively correlated to current life satisfaction. In other words, respondents who rated highly on all three historical dimensions of importance (i.e., importance to the individual) also indicated a greater sense of present well-being. In predicting future optimism, however, only national resilience, albeit marginally, correlated to future satisfaction; respondents who rated highly the historical events associated with resilience were more upbeat about the future.

IMPLICATIONS FOR THE SINGAPORE STORY

What does it mean for the future of Singapore? The findings suggest that the Singapore Story has become a shared representation of history. Events that are not experienced directly but are critical to the development of the Singapore Story have been weaved into the consciousness of the populace. For the historical narrative to be meaningful, it has to reach out to and inspire confidence among ordinary Singaporeans, and this is seen in the episodes of history that celebrate the Singapore spirit.

The theme of overcoming the odds resonates well with the population. Events that embody the spirit of resilience highlight the perseverance and conviction of Singaporeans. National resilience emphasises how the nation rallies together in the face of domestic or international challenges and crises. These include tackling national tragedies (e.g., the cable car accident), surmounting challenges (e.g., hosting the inaugural Youth Olympic Games) and prevailing against threats (e.g., international repercussions following the caning of Michael Fay). These are lessons that can be weaved into the Singapore Story.

The population, however, might focus on particular aspects of the story over others. Respondents were either not aware of certain critical events or were aware of the events but did not perceive them as important. Take, for example, the "Marxist Conspiracy" (18.5% aware, mean score of 3.29 on importance to respondent) and the bombing of MacDonald House (52.6% aware, mean score of 3.48 on importance to respondent). The reason may be because these events affected one group more than another. For instance, the "Marxist Conspiracy" to subvert government authorities had direct implications to the religious community in Singapore, and hence resonated more strongly among those who were aware of it.

Paradoxically, while people are seemingly more aware of economic events (e.g., the opening of the two casinos and the Asian Financial Crisis) than political developments or infrastructure breakthroughs (e.g., the formation of PAP or the completion of the NEWater plant), the latter is regarded as more important even though the former is generally accepted as an integral aspect of the Singapore Story. It may be that economic events, on the whole, have had relatively limited impact on Singaporeans compared with events that centred on politics or infrastructure building. Singapore, for instance, weathered the

Asian Financial Crisis better than other Asian countries (Ngiam & ISEAS, 2000;[43] Tan, 2001).[44] Yet, capacity building such as the ramping up of transportation services was often entangled in politics and, hence, the latter might seem to have wider-ranging impact.

Last but not least, events loaded on the differences factor highlight the fault lines and contestations in our history. The opening of the two casinos (2010), the PAP losing Aljunied GRC (2011), the major MRT breakdown (2011) and the escape of Mas Selamat (2008) are recent events that were classified as thematically similar to our controversial past such as the racial riots, school streaming and the bilingualism policy. While all of them were considered socially divisive — hence the label "differences" — the first group of events seems to suggest a decline in public confidence as reflected by the breakdown of the public transport system, a security lapse and the changes in political fortune. It remains to be seen if the erosion in competent governance will be a protracted one.

The list of events in the nation-building and national resilience narratives is related to the perception of present well-being but not so much for future well-being. National resilience is linked, albeit marginally, to an optimistic future. However, the success of the Singapore Story is premised on the acceptance of a narrative that forges a sense of common destiny (Ho, 2014),[45] not just the sense of well-being. Understanding which influential stories can impact social cohesion will shed light on the next chapter of the Singapore Story.

Lastly, national education has been valuable in the transmission of the representation and physical symbols have been effective in reinforcing the sense of nationhood and our shared destiny. It might, however, be difficult to have a single shared representation of events as residents have different age and racial reference points. Older Singaporeans share a deeper imprint of Singapore's developmental history, be that the tribulations or triumphant moments in our shared memory of the city-state. For younger Singaporeans, the historical

---

[43] Ngiam, K. J., & Institute of Southeast Asian Studies. (2000). *Coping with the Asian Financial Crisis: The Singapore experience.* Singapore: Institute of Southeast Asian Studies.

[44] Tan, H. H. A. (2001). The Asian Economic Crisis: The Way Ahead for Singapore. In L. Low, & D. M. Johnston (Eds.), *Singapore Inc: Public policy options in the third millennium* (pp. 17–34). Singapore: Asia Pacific Press.

[45] Ho, op. cit.

events and lessons learnt will inevitably be eroded as time passes by. It is important to determine how the Singapore Story is to be remembered, shared and disserted as the divergence of interests across generations could result in fragmented identities.

THE NEW SINGAPORE NARRATIVE

Singapore would not have survived the tribulations of the last century without the unwavering support of its people. The city state that was once deemed an improbable nation has overcome insurmountable odds to emerge as a first-world nation in a single generation. The narratives promulgated over the past 50 years offer a glimpse into our subconscious sense of nationhood (i.e., nation-building) while, at the same time, highlight the policies, events and calamities that define our social fractures (i.e., differences) and the shared memories of how we forged ahead in spite of the difficulties encountered (i.e., national resilience). These historical narratives are collective memories that bind Singaporeans, and will be a source of inspiration to successive generations of Singaporeans.

The passing of Mr Lee Kuan Yew in March 2015 marked the end of an era for the pioneers of Singapore. The world that Singaporeans inherit will be increasingly unpredictable and less benign. And while the common narratives are anchors to our shared values and ethos, future generations of Singaporeans will need to chart their own chronicles even as they rely on the historical milestones as a signpost to the next unknown. Historical events will be reviewed and re-interpreted based on contemporary thought paradigm — the revisionist perspective on the legitimacy of Operation Cold Store in recent years is a case in point (*The Straits Times*, April 13, 2015).[46] One hundred and seven people were detained in the 1963 island-wide security crackdown allegedly for communist subversions. Younger historians now question if the arrests were politically motivated, and if the threats of communism had been exaggerated. What type of narratives should be promulgated for the next 50 years? What should be the new Singapore narratives? These will be the

---

[46] *The Straits Times* (2015, April 13). Revisiting Operation Coldstore. Retrieved from http://www.straitstimes.com/news/opinion/more-opinion-stories/story/revisiting-operation-coldstore-20150413.

questions for scholars and policymakers to ponder over as we embark on the next chapter of the Singapore Story.

CONCLUSION

In summary, the current study examines how Singaporeans view 50 key historical events in terms of awareness, perceived importance, evaluation and emotional resonance. This piece of uncharted research offers valuable insights and introspection into understanding how history is socially constructed, and distils the dominant narratives that shape nationhood and well-being. Singapore's nation-building journey shall always remain a work in progress. Historical memories will provide the best value compass for Singapore to navigate forward in an ever complex and changing environment.

About the Contributors

CHAN Chun Sing is currently Minister in the Prime Minister's Office and Secretary-General of the National Trades Union Congress. On 1 October 2015, he was appointed Deputy Chairman of the People's Association. On 8 April 2015, the NTUC Central Committee unanimously elected him to be NTUC Secretary-General from 4 May 2015 to help strengthen labour leadership at NTUC and the link between the Labour Movement and the Government. He was re-elected as the NTUC Secretary-General by the NTUC National Delegates' Conference on 29 October 2015.

On 9 April 2015, Mr Chan was appointed Minister in the Prime Minister's Office and relinquished his appointments as Minister for Social and Family Development and Second Minister for Defence, both of which he has held since 1 September 2013. As Minister for Social and Family Development, Mr Chan was responsible for improving social service delivery, enhancing social safety nets and strengthening support for families in Singapore. His previous appointments included Acting Minister for Community Development, Youth and Sports, and Minister of State for Information, Communications and the Arts.

Mr Chan has been twice elected to the Parliament in the Tanjong Pagar Group Representation Constituency (GRC) in the General Elections of 2011 and 2015. Educated at the Raffles Institution (1982–1985) and Raffles Junior College (1986–1987), he was awarded the SAF (Overseas) and President's Scholarship to study Economics at Christ's College, Cambridge University in the United Kingdom in 1988 and graduated with First Class Honours. In 2005, he completed the Sloan Fellows Programme at the Massachusetts Institute of Technology under the Lee Kuan Yew Scholarship.

Magdalene CHOO was a Research Associate at the Institute of Policy Studies (IPS). Her key contributions were in the design and implementation of the Singapore Panel Study of Social Dynamics, a study devised to track changes in 5,000 households over time. She was seconded to IPS from the National Security Coordination Secretariat, where her responsibilities included co-ordinating resilience policy and research as well as leading risk assessment and horizon scanning efforts. Magdalene has a BA (Psychology & Philosophy) from the National University of Singapore (NUS) and an MA (Psychology) from New Zealand's University of Otago. She is currently pursuing her PhD (Psychology) at NUS.

Janadas DEVAN, Director of the Institute of Policy Studies, was educated at the National University of Singapore and Cornell University in the United States. He was a journalist, writing for *The Straits Times* and broadcasting for Radio Singapore International, before being appointed the Government's Chief of Communications at the Ministry of Communications and Information in 2012.

Evelyn GOH is the Shedden Professor of Strategic Policy Studies at the Australian National University. She has published widely on US-China relations and diplomatic history, East Asian security and institutions, Southeast Asian strategies towards great powers, and environmental security. Her latest books are *The Struggle for Order: Hegemony, Hierarchy and Transition in Post-Cold War East Asia* (Oxford University Press, 2013 and 2015 paperback), and *Rising China's Influence in Developing Asia* (Oxford University Press, 2016). She has held previous faculty positions at the Universities of Oxford and London, and the S. Rajaratnam School of International Studies in Singapore. She holds Master and Doctoral degrees in International Relations and an undergraduate degree in Geography, all from Oxford.

HO Qiao Ying Elaine is a Research Analyst at the Institute of Policy Studies (IPS), Social Lab. Prior to this, she was Research Assistant at the Faculty of Arts and Social Sciences, National University of Singapore (NUS). Her research interests are in ageing, family and health. She is currently working on the Singapore Panel Study on Social Dynamics, a flagship project of IPS Social

Lab. Her published work includes op-ed articles for TODAY and IPS Commons. She graduated with a BSocSci (Honours) in Sociology from NUS.

HOE Su Fern is currently Research Fellow at the Institute of Policy Studies. She is working on two cultural policy projects funded by the National Arts Council, Singapore: (i) arts housing and creative placemaking in Singapore and (ii) scoping community arts in Singapore. She also supports the IPS Director in his research and publications.

Dr Hoe received her PhD from the University of Melbourne in 2011. Her thesis focused on the governance of the creative industries in Singapore and Taiwan. Prior to joining IPS, she held appointments at the Ministry of Communications and Information as well as the Supreme Court. She has also taught in the areas of Cultural Studies, Communication Design and Media and Communications in Singapore and Australia.

Bilahari KAUSIKAN retired in June 2013 and is currently Ambassador-at-Large and Policy Adviser in the Ministry of Foreign Affairs (MFA). From 2001 to May 2013, Ambassador Kausikan was first the Second Permanent Secretary and then Permanent Secretary of MFA. He had previously served in a variety of appointments in the Ministry and as the Permanent Representative to the United Nations in New York and as Ambassador to the Russian Federation.

Raffles Institution, the University of Singapore and Columbia University in New York all attempted to educate him.

Vikram KHANNA is Associate Editor of *The Business Times*, where he has worked since 1993. Prior to that he was an Economist at the International Monetary Fund in Washington DC, United States, where he spent seven years. A Singaporean, Mr Khanna has spent more than 28 years of his life in Singapore. During that time, he has served on several government committees, including the Economic Review Committee of 2001, the Pro-Enterprise Panel and The Enterprise Challenge. He is a prolific writer and has conducted more than 200 full-length interviews with global Chief Executive Officers, government leaders and thought leaders from around the world.

Mr Khanna serves on the Board of The Substation, an independent arts centre, and is on the Council of the Economic Society of Singapore. He has

BA, MA and MPhil degrees in Economics from the University of Cambridge, United Kingdom.

LEONG Chan-Hoong is Deputy Head, Social Lab and Senior Research Fellow at the Institute of Policy Studies (IPS). His research interests include immigration and integration, historical narratives and identity, and the management of workplace diversity. He was Consulting Editor for the *International Journal of Intercultural Relations* (2013–2015), and Editor for the 2013 Special Issue, "Multiculturalism: Beyond Ethnocultural Diversity and Contestations". He is Principal Investigator for the IPS survey on National Service (commissioned by the Committee to Strengthen National Service); the Applied Study in Polytechnics and ITE Review (Commissioned by the Ministry of Education); and the Panel Study on Social Dynamics (Commissioned by the Resilience Policy and Research Centre). Dr Leong is a panel member of the Research and Advisory Board at the National Council of Social Service.

Linda LIM has written on Singapore's economy since 1976, with her latest academic articles appearing in 2014 and 2015. A Professor of Strategy at the Stephen M. Ross School of Business at the University of Michigan (U-M), teaching MBA and executive courses on the World Economy and Business in Asia, she was Director of U-M's Center for Southeast Asian Studies from 2005 to 2009. With degrees in economics from Cambridge (BA), Yale (MA) and Michigan (PhD), she has published extensively on international trade, investment, industrial policy, labour and business in Asia. A former Trustee of Asia Society and long-time Board Member of the Knight-Wallace Fellows, Professor Lim has consulted for many multinational companies, government and international agencies and think-tanks. She has served, and serves, as an Independent Director of two US public companies in the technology space with extensive Asian operations.

Varian LIM is Research Analyst at the Institute of Policy Studies (IPS). Prior to joining IPS, Varian worked at the National Institute of Education as a research assistant, where he was involved in a project investigating the attention profiles of secondary school students. He has work experience in diverse areas such as the performing arts and events coordination. He graduated from SIM University (UniSIM) with a First Class in Psychology. He was also awarded Best Experimental Research for his honours thesis at the Singapore Psychological Society (SPS) Student Research Awards in 2012.

Kishore MAHBUBANI has had the good fortune of enjoying a career in government and, at the same time, in writing extensively on public issues. He was with the Singapore Foreign Service for 33 years (1971–2004) where he had postings in Cambodia, Malaysia, Washington DC and New York, where he served two postings as Singapore's Ambassador to the UN and as President of the UN Security Council in January 2001 and May 2002. He was Permanent Secretary at the Foreign Ministry from 1993 to 1998. Currently, he is the Dean and Professor in the Practice of Public Policy at the Lee Kuan Yew School of Public Policy of the National University of Singapore. In the world of ideas, he has spoken and published globally. His latest book is *The Great Convergence: Asia, the West, and the Logic of One World*, was selected by *The Financial Times* as one of the best books of 2013.

Paveena SEAH has been Research Analyst at the Institute of Policy Studies (IPS) Social Lab since 2014. She has a Masters in Ageing and Society from the Institute of Gerontology, King's College London. Prior to joining IPS, Ms Seah worked at the People's Association where she was responsible for the development and implementation of the Mountbatten Wellness Programme. Her research interests include social and healthcare policies for older adults, intergenerational relations and heritage management in Singapore. Her published work includes op-ed articles for *TODAY* and IPS Commons. She is currently working on the Singapore Panel Study on Social Dynamics.

Carol SOON is Research Fellow at the Institute of Policy Studies (IPS). Her research interests include digital engagement, how individuals and organisations leverage new media to engender political and social change, and subaltern discourses and communities online. She is working on a study on the use of media and the Internet during General Election 2015.

Her research has been published in peer-reviewed journals, including Journal of Computer-Mediated Communication, Information Communication

& Society, Asian Journal of Communication, Journal of Information Technology and Politics, and Social Science and Computer Review, and three book projects. Dr Soon has taught courses in advanced communication and media research, and culture industries at the Department of Communications and New Media. She is currently teaching a module on new media and politics at the University Scholars Programme in NUS.

Prior to joining academia, she was in the corporate sector where she developed communication campaigns for profit and non-profit organisations. Dr Soon is also Member of the Media Literacy Council and Associate Editor of *Media Asia Journal*.

Debra SOON is responsible for the programming, branding, marketing and distribution of Channel NewsAsia, *TODAY* and 938Live, including their digital platforms channelnewsasia.com and TODAYonline.com. She has taken on these portfolios in a streamlining of the company's activities to sharpen its focus on customers. She oversees the enhancement of these news products and their commercial value.

With over 20 years of experience in the media and communications industry, Ms Soon was appointed Managing Director of Channel NewsAsia in March 2009. She was responsible then for the editorial for English, Chinese, Malay and Tamil news and current affairs, as well as the business operations of Channel NewsAsia.

Ms Soon is a mentor/member of BoardAgender and an executive committee member of the Singapore Committee for UN Women, formerly known as UNIFEM Singapore. She is also on the Business Advisory Board of the Behavioural Sciences Institute of the Singapore Management University.

Ms Soon obtained her BSc (Econs) and MSc in International Relations from the London School of Economics and Political Science under scholarship from the Singapore Broadcasting Corporation, and later the Television Corporation of Singapore.

Eugene K B TAN is Associate Professor of Law at the Singapore Management University (SMU). He also co-directs the SMU Centre for Scholars' Development.

Associate Professor Tan was educated at the National University of Singapore, the London School of Economics and Political Science, and Stanford University where he was a Fulbright Fellow. He was admitted to the Singapore Bar in 1996.

His inter-disciplinary research interests and teaching portfolio (in SMU's law, business, and social sciences schools) include law and public policy; constitutional and administrative law; the regulation of ethnic conflict; ethics and social responsibility; and the government and politics of Singapore. Between February 2012 and August 2014, Associate Professor Tan served as a Nominated Member of Parliament in Singapore's 12th Parliament.

TAN Kong Yam is presently Professor of Economics at Nanyang Technological University and the Co-Director of the Asia Competitiveness Institute at the Lee Kuan Yew School of Public Policy, National University of Singapore.

From 1985 to 1988, he was the Chief Assistant to Dr Goh Keng Swee, the former Deputy Prime Minister of Singapore invited by Mr Deng Xiaoping to advise China on economic development strategy. From 2002 to 2005, he was a Senior Economist at the World Bank office in Beijing. Prior to that, Professor Tan was the Chief Economist of the Singapore government (1999–2002) and Head of Department of Business Policy at NUS Business School. He served as Board Member at the Central Provident Fund Board (1984–1996), National Productivity Board (1989–1990), and CapitaMalls Asia (2009–2014). He has also consulted for many organisations including Temasek, GIC, Citigroup and CapitaLand.

Professor Tan's research interests include international trade and finance; economic and business trends in the Asia Pacific region; and economic reforms in China. Professor Tan has published 10 books and numerous articles in major international publications.

Professor Tan graduated from Princeton and Stanford University.

TEO Chee Hean was appointed Deputy Prime Minister on 1 April 2009. He also serves, since 21 May 2011, as Co-ordinating Minister for National Security. He is also Minister in charge of the Civil Service. He oversees the National Population and Talent Division and the National Climate Change Secretariat, and is Chairman of the National Research Foundation.

In the first phase of his career, he served in the Singapore Armed Forces (SAF) where he held various command and staff appointments in the Republic of Singapore Navy and the Joint Staff. In 1991, he was appointed Chief of Navy, and was promoted to the rank of Rear Admiral. In December 1992, he left the SAF to seek elected public office and was elected as a Member of Parliament in a by-election in the Marine Parade Group Representation Constituency (GRC). He was re-elected to Parliament five times in the Pasir Ris-Punggol GRC.

He has served as the Minister for Home Affairs, Minister for Defence, Minister for Education, and Minister for the Environment. He has also served as Minister of State in the Ministries of Finance, Communications and Defence.

TONG Yee co-founded the School of Thought (SOT) to promote innovation in education and civic learning in both private and public sectors. SOT has since evolved to become The Thought Collective (TTC) — a group of social enterprises reputed for building social and emotional capital and are at the forefront of social innovation in Singapore. Other companies under TTC comprise Think Tank Studio, Thinkscape, Food for Thought, and Common Ground. As a social innovator, Mr Tong provides consultancy for national agencies such as the National Council of Social Service and NEXUS. He also spearheaded civic initiatives such as the Stand Up for Singapore Movement, Economic Development Board's 50th Anniversary Business Innovation Learning Summit, and Youthopia Youth Mentorship Movement. Some of his current endeavours include prototyping a sustainable volunteer programme, designing thought-provoking educational experiences through trail innovation, and initiating compelling social movements in hope of creating a more gracious society. A champion of social emotional learning and ontological coaching, Mr Tong is a highly sought-after motivational speaker and trainer. Mr Tong also sits on a number of national committees. He is a council member of the National Youth Council, S50 Committee (Education and Youth) and Advisory Committee for Youth Corps Singapore.

YANG Wai Wai is Associate Director at the Institute of Policy Studies (IPS). Prior to joining the Institute, she was Deputy Director at the Earth

Observatory of Singapore, where she conducted strategic research and planning related to the Observatory's development and advancement. She was in the publishing industry and worked in The Economist Intelligence Unit and Thomson Financial Services as an editor, before joining the National University of Singapore. Prior to that, she was a research analyst at Singapore's Ministry of Defence. She has a Masters in International Relations from Yale University, and a Bachelor of Arts (Honours) in Social and Political Sciences from the University of Cambridge.

www.ingramcontent.com/pod-product-compliance
Lightning Source LLC
Chambersburg PA
CBHW050649280326
41932CB00015B/2836